THE LUXURY BIBLE

THE LUXURY BIBLE

The Conditions *of* Power

LUXORAE™

THE LUXURY BIBLE
Alignment Authority and Inheritance

Written by Luxorae™

THE LUXURY BIBLE
The Conditions of Power © 2026 Luxorae™

All rights reserved. Published under the brand name Luxorae™ Luxorae™ is a trademark of Luxorae™ LLC

No part of this book may be reproduced, stored in a retrieval system, or transmitted in any form or by any means—electronic, mechanical, photocopying, recording, or otherwise—without the prior written permission of the copyright holder, except for brief quotations used in reviews or scholarly analysis.

This book is a work of original thought and expression. Any resemblance to existing works, living or dead, is coincidental and non-derivative. The frameworks, language, and concepts presented herein—including but not limited to "Alignment Sovereignty," "The Luxury Bible," and "Luxorae™", Luxorae LLC—are the intellectual property of Amercia Morris.

ISBN: 979-8-9947700-0-9

First Edition Published by: Luxorae™ LLC Buffalo, NY, USA
www.LuxoraeLife.com
Printed in the United States of America

DISCLAIMER

This book is not intended to replace professional psychological, medical, legal, or financial advice. The material is presented for educational and reflective purposes only. The author and publisher disclaim any liability arising directly or indirectly from the application of ideas contained herein.

DEDICATION

This book is dedicated to those who learned how to survive long before they were taught how to rest.

To the ones who inherited discipline before delight, responsibility before ease, and resilience before reassurance. To those whose families taught them how to endure systems that were never designed with their wholeness in mind—and who carried that endurance with dignity, even when it came at great personal cost.

It is also dedicated to those standing at the threshold between gratitude and growth. To those who honor what their elders survived, while quietly sensing that inheritance must mean more than endurance alone. To those who feel the tension between loyalty and longing, faith and clarity, humility and self-trust.

Finally, this book is for those ready to reclaim sovereignty without rejection. For those who understand that survival was never the destination. It was the bridge.

May this work help you remember that ease is not a betrayal of struggle—it is its fulfillment.

— **Luxorae**™

LETTER FROM THE AUTHOR

Dear Reader,

I did not write this book to be liked.

I wrote it because I watched too many brilliant, capable, deeply faithful people—particularly what's Classified as Black Americans—live and die without ever experiencing the freedom they prayed for, worked for, and deserved.

I watched them hustle until their bodies broke. I watched them give until there was nothing left. I watched them wait for permission that never came. And I watched systems benefit from their labor, loyalty, and silence—while offering them scraps dressed up as progress.

I also watched something else.

I watched people who seemed to move differently. Calmer. Clearer. Less burdened. Not because they had more money, more faith, or better circumstances—but because they had something **internal** that the rest of us had been taught to distrust: **sovereignty**.

This book is my attempt to make that internal shift **teachable**.

Not as mysticism. Not as self-help. But as **structure**.

Because I believe—deeply, after years of study, observation, and lived experience—that most of us were never taught the difference between survival and freedom. We were taught to endure, to comply, to wait, to sacrifice. And those teachings kept people alive. I honor that.

But survival was never supposed to be the destination. It was the bridge.

And too many of us are still standing on it—calling it home.

This book is not for everyone.
It is not for people who need external validation to move.
It is not for people who prefer comfort over clarity.
It is not for people who want to be told what to think.

This book is for people who are **tired**—but not broken.

Tired of performing.
Tired of waiting.
Tired of living in contradiction.

It is for people ready to ask hard questions:
- What if the frameworks I inherited were designed for someone else's benefit?
- What if freedom requires something different than what I was taught?
- What if I am more capable than I've been allowed to believe?

If those questions make you uncomfortable, **good**. That discomfort is recognition, not resistance.

A FEW THINGS BEFORE YOU BEGIN:

This book will reference scripture, philosophy, psychology, and history—not to overwhelm you, but to show you that what I'm saying is not new.

It's been said across traditions, time periods, and cultures. It's just been **buried, adapted, or controlled** by institutions.

I'm not asking you to abandon your faith, your culture, or your people. I'm asking you to reclaim the **internal authority** those things were always meant to protect.

This book will challenge inherited beliefs—not out of disrespect, but out of love. Because the people who taught you survival strategies did the best they could with what they had. Now you have access to something they didn't: **the time and space to build for freedom instead of endurance**.

And finally: I do not have all the answers. I am not a guru. I am not your savior.

I am someone who saw a pattern, tested it, lived it, and decided it was too valuable not to share.

What you do with it is up to you.

THANK YOU FOR BEING HERE.

Whether you finish this book or stop halfway through, whether you agree with everything or argue with half of it—**thank you for showing up**.

That willingness to engage, to question, to sit with discomfort—that's already sovereignty in motion.

The rest is just practice.

With respect and clarity,

Luxorae™
Buffalo, New York
January 2026

EPIGRAPH

LIBERATION

TRUTH

"And you shall know the truth, and the truth shall make you free."
— John 8:32

ORDER

"Order is not pressure. It is peace."
— Luxorae™

PREFACE

A BOOK THAT REFUSES EASY CATEGORIES

This book will be misunderstood by some.

Not because it is reckless, hostile, or deliberately provocative—but because it refuses to sit comfortably inside any single institution, ideology, or tradition. It does not attack religion, nor does it defend it. It does not reject liberation movements, nor does it romanticize them. It does not promise escape, nor does it sanctify suffering.

It insists on something more demanding: **clarity**.

Many readers have been trained—by history, education, and theology—to assume that authority must come from outside the self. As a result, any framework that restores internal authority is quickly labeled dangerous, arrogant, or heretical. This reaction is not new. It has followed every serious attempt to reconnect truth with lived experience rather than institutional permission.

This book does not claim to replace scripture, tradition, or collective struggle. It claims something far more modest—and far more disruptive:

That reality responds most consistently to internal alignment, not external belief.

This is not theological dogma.
It is an observable pattern across philosophy, psychology, history, and human experience.

When this book references the Bible, the Bhagavad Gita, Black liberation leaders, or philosophical thinkers, it does not attempt to collapse them into a single belief system. It highlights **convergence**—the repeated appearance of the same structural truth across cultures and centuries.

This book is not asking you to believe something new.
It is asking you to **notice something ancient**.

If this work feels uncomfortable, it is likely because it removes familiar shortcuts:
- Obedience without understanding
- Belief without embodiment
- Liberation without responsibility

In their place, it introduces alignment, authorship, and internal governance.

That shift can feel threatening—not because it is wrong, but because it places responsibility where it has long been avoided.

Read this book slowly.
Do not look for agreement.
Look for **coherence**.

If something resonates, test it.
If something resists, examine why.

This book does not demand allegiance.
It invites **alignment**.

WHY LUXURY WAS NEVER THE GOAL

Luxury has been sold to us as an object—something to acquire, display, or escape into. We were taught to associate it with money, status, and excess, while being quietly trained to distrust the very source from which luxury actually emerges: **sovereignty**.

This book begins with a correction.

Luxury is not excess.
Luxury is not indulgence.
Luxury is not permission granted by systems or institutions.

Luxury is sovereignty—the condition of internal alignment in which a person governs their own mind, energy, labor, and direction without contradiction.

Where sovereignty exists, provision follows.
Where sovereignty is absent, extraction takes place.

This is not motivational language. It is historical, spiritual, and structural fact.

Luxury, in its truest sense, is not expensiveness but wholeness. It is the absence of internal fracture—the condition in which one's time, energy, values, and direction are no longer in conflict. Luxury is peace that does not require escape, abundance that does not require excess, and stability that does not depend on external validation.

Lavishness, in this context, is not display but sufficiency: the ability to move through life without urgency, scarcity thinking, or self-betrayal. Where sovereignty governs the inner life, luxury appears naturally—not as spectacle, but as ease, clarity, and continuity.

Empires did not become wealthy because they were virtuous. They became wealthy because they assumed authority. Land, labor, and resources have always moved toward those who believed—internally and collectively—that they had the right to govern reality.

The injustice of this history is undeniable.
But embedded within it is a principle that cannot be ignored:

RESOURCES FOLLOW POWER, NOT PERMISSION.

The tragedy is that generations of people—particularly those descended from the exploited—were later taught a theology, an education, and a psychology that disconnected them from this principle. They were encouraged to seek abundance while being discouraged from sovereignty. They were taught to pursue wealth while being trained to distrust themselves.

This contradiction produced dependency.

God was placed "out there."
Power was placed "up there."
Value was placed "somewhere else."

Meanwhile, patience, humility, obedience, and waiting were framed as virtue.

Yet scripture quietly contradicts this arrangement:

"The kingdom of God is within you."
"As a man thinketh in his heart, so is he."
"You shall know the truth, and the truth shall make you free."

These are not poetic metaphors.
They describe **mechanism**.

This book is not about becoming wealthy for its own sake. It is about removing the distortions that make wealth—and peace, clarity, authority, and sufficiency—feel distant, conditional, or undeserved.

You are not seeking luxury.
You are reclaiming **inheritance**.

CONTENTS

LETTER FROM THE AUTHOR ix

EPIGRAPH xii
PREFACE xiii
READER'S GUIDE xxii
PROLOGUE.. xxiii

PART I: REDEFINING LUXURY 1

CHAPTER 1... 3
"Luxury is not excess. It is the absence of unnecessary friction."

INTERLUDE... 10

PART II: FEAR, POWER, AND IDENTITY 17

CHAPTER 2 19
"Fear works best when it feels like wisdom."

CHAPTER 3 28
"Power does not begin when permission is granted."

CHAPTER 4 36
"Belief is not a substitute for self-trust."

PART II: FEAR, POWER, AND IDENTITY (Continued) 43

CHAPTER 5 .... **45**
"Identity is the infrastructure of every outcome."

BEYOND THE HIERARCHY 54
"Needs do not upgrade identity. Alignment does."

CHAPTER 6 .... **60**
"Identity is rebuilt through repetition, not revelation."

PART II: FEAR, POWER, AND IDENTITY (Continued) 71

INTERLUDE **73**

PART III: INHERITANCE, NOT REBELLION **81**

CHAPTER 7 .... **83**
"Money exposes alignment. It does not create it."

INTERLUDE **93**
How Adapted Frameworks Became "Facts"—and
Why You Can Set the Standard

PART IV: CONVERGENCE ACROSS TRADITIONS **99**

INTERLUDE **101**

INTERLUDE **107**

INTERLUDE **114**

AUTHOR'S NOTE ON POLARITY **120**

PART V: SOURCE, POLARITY, AND CONTINUITY 123

CHAPTER 8 125
"Authority survives where belief is protected."

CHAPTER 9 134
"Source does not ask for permission."

CHAPTER 10 143
"Care is not weakness; it is continuity."

PART V: SOURCE, POLARITY, AND CONTINUITY (Continued) 151

CHAPTER 11 153
"Protection is love in motion."

PART VI: ALIGNMENT IN MOTION 163

CHAPTER 12 165
"Reality responds to structure, not wishes."

CHAPTER 13 174
"Alignment is relational."

PART VI: ALIGNMENT IN MOTION (Continued) 183

CHAPTER 14 185
"Patterns are not miracles."

CHAPTER 15 196
"Skepticism is not the enemy. Vagueness is."

PART VII: UNLEARNING, TRUST, AND FREEDOM **205**

CHAPTER 16 .... **207**
"Survival wisdom is not the same as freedom truth."

PART VII: UNLEARNING, TRUST, AND FREEDOM (Continued) **215**

CHAPTER 17 .... **217**
"Freedom is an outcome, not a promise."

PART VIII: UNION & CLOSURE **227**

CHAPTER 18 .... **229**
"Recognition always comes before change."

EPILOGUE **235**

WORKBOOK **240**

MASTER APPENDIX **246**

FORMAL BIBLIOGRAPHY **263**

ABOUT LUXORAE™ **265**

A FINAL INVITATION **266**

READER'S GUIDE

HOW TO USE THIS BOOK

This book is not designed to be consumed quickly or passively. It is meant to be **worked with**.

The value is not in agreement.
The value is in **alignment**.

How to Engage:
- **Read slowly. Pause often.**
- **Notice resistance**; it signals conditioning, not failure.
- **Do not rush to apply**—first understand.
- **Revisit sections** as your perspective shifts.

This is not linear information.
It is structural recalibration.

Each chapter includes:
- **A core principle** (chapter epigraph)
- **Conceptual framework**
- **A reflection moment** (personal recognition)
- **A recurring question** (to sit with)
- **Practice for integration** (where applicable)

Some chapters are brief and conceptual.
Others are longer and include exercises.

Trust the rhythm.

PROLOGUE

THE COST OF FORGETTING WHO GOVERNS YOU

There is a form of poverty that has nothing to do with money.

It is the poverty of **self-distrust**.

It appears when people doubt their own perception, outsource judgment, and move through life seeking permission to exist fully. It is reinforced when fear is normalized and obedience is spiritualized. It thrives when identity is obscured.

This poverty is profitable.

Entire systems depend on it. Institutions are stabilized by it. Economies function because large numbers of people are trained to doubt their own authority while generating value for others.

Fear is the primary tool.
Fear of being wrong.
Fear of rejection.
Fear of losing access.
Fear of stepping outside what is sanctioned.

Yet fear is neither neutral nor divine.

Scripture is explicit: *"God has not given us a spirit of fear."*

Fear signals misalignment. It emerges when people forget who governs their lives and begin living according to external definitions of worth, success, and legitimacy.

History shows the result:
People with immense capacity become compliant.
Communities rich in creativity become extractive zones.
Power is surrendered—and renamed humility.

But something else is also true.

When people remember who they are, fear loses leverage.
When internal authority is restored, behavior changes without force.

Presence shifts.
Decisions clarify.
Energy stops leaking into performance and explanation.

This is the authority that does not announce itself.
This is the coherence that cannot be faked.

Luxury emerges here—not as spectacle, but as peace, time, clarity, and sufficiency.

Provision follows the presence of "the Glow"

Money responds because money is a follower.
It always has been.

A QUESTION WE WERE NEVER ENCOURAGED TO ASK

We are taught that truth requires sources.
That credibility depends on origin, authorship, and preservation.

Yet when it comes to the systems governing our beliefs, faith, and identity, we are rarely encouraged to apply that same rigor.

So here is the invitation:

Ask where this began.
Ask who benefited.
Ask why it was passed down—unchallenged.

This book does not ask for blind agreement.
It offers history, scripture, context, and evidence many were never given access to.

We were taught—formally, academically, rigorously—that truth requires verification. That every claim must be traced. That credibility depends on *where something began, who authored it, and why it was preserved.*

Yet when it comes to the systems that govern our beliefs, our faith, and our identity, we are rarely encouraged to apply that same discipline.

So before moving forward, ask yourself:
- Where did this teaching originate?
- Who benefited from its preservation?
- Why was it passed down without interrogation?

If you choose to continue reading, understand this:
This book is not asking for blind agreement.

It is offering the sources, the history, the scripture, and the context that many were never given access to.

The answers exist.
The evidence exists.
The history exists.

The question is whether you are willing to look.

PART I:
REDEFINING LUXURY

CHAPTER 1

"Luxury is not excess. It is the absence of unnecessary friction."

Luxury, Misdefined

Luxury has always been easier to sell than sovereignty.

Objects can be displayed. Status can be measured. Excess can be admired or resented. But sovereignty—internal authority, self-governance, and alignment between belief and action—cannot be easily commodified. So it was rebranded, obscured, and replaced with symbols.

Over time, luxury became associated with accumulation rather than freedom, appearance rather than peace, and consumption rather than control of one's life. The shift was subtle, but consequential: people were trained to pursue outcomes while neglecting the condition that produces them.

Luxury was turned into a destination rather than a state of being.

Yet history is clear: luxury has rarely belonged to those who worked the hardest or waited the longest. It has belonged to those who governed themselves—and, often, by extension, others. Time, comfort, and security were not rewards. They were consequences of authority.

That is why redefining luxury matters.

THE TRUE DEFINITION

Luxury, in its true sense, is not extravagance. It is margin.

It is the ability to decide without panic.
To rest without guilt.
To move without fear.
To create without begging.

Luxury is space—mentally, emotionally, materially—because your life is not governed by constant reaction.

This is why people can earn large sums of money and still live without luxury. Their minds remain anxious. Their decisions remain reactive. Their time remains controlled by external demands. Wealth without sovereignty produces stress, not freedom.

And this is why some people with modest resources live with unmistakable ease. They possess clarity, autonomy, and self-trust. Their lives are governed from the inside out.

The modern world reverses this order. It teaches people to chase money first and hope peace arrives later. But peace does not arrive as a result of accumulation. Peace emerges when internal conflict is resolved.

Scripture quietly affirms this inversion:

"Better is a little with righteousness than great revenues without right."
— **Proverbs 16:8**

This is not a condemnation of wealth. It is a warning about misalignment.

SOVEREIGNTY PRODUCES LUXURY

Luxury is the absence of internal contradiction.

When thoughts, values, actions, and direction become coherent, energy stops leaking. Decisions simplify. Relationships clarify. Work becomes more effective. Over time, resources respond—not because you demanded them, but because coherence is attractive.

This is why money follows sovereignty.
Money is not an initiator. It is a responder. It moves toward clarity, competence, and confidence. It avoids chaos, desperation, and internal division. Even unjust systems reward those who know who they are—because reliability is valuable everywhere.

This truth is uncomfortable because it removes excuses. It places responsibility where it belongs: on internal governance.

But it is also liberating.

If luxury were merely external, it would always be scarce.
If luxury required permission, it could always be withheld.
But if luxury is sovereignty, then it is recoverable—immediately, internally, and without approval.

This book begins here because no amount of strategy, faith, or effort can compensate for misalignment. Before wealth can be stewarded, authority must be reclaimed. Before inheritance can be enjoyed, identity must be remembered.

Luxury was never lost.
It was misdefined.

A MOMENT YOU RECOGNIZE

You watched someone with less money move through life with more ease.

You couldn't explain it, but you noticed it.

That was your first clue.

Recurring Question (implicit):
What if luxury was never about accumulation?

Alignment Exercise: Internal Audit
Complete these sentences without editing yourself:

- "I feel most free when I am _____."
- "I feel least sovereign when I am _____."
- "I often give my authority away to _____."
- "If I trusted myself fully, I would _____."

This is not for judgment. It is for clarity.

Practice for the Week
Daily Decision Filter
Before each major decision, ask:
"Does this increase my sovereignty or my dependency?"

Choose accordingly.

KEY PRINCIPLE TO CARRY FORWARD

Luxury is not something you chase.
Luxury is something you stabilize.

Stabilize your mind.
Stabilize your identity.
Stabilize your direction.

Resources will respond.

CLOSING NOTE TO THE READER

If this chapter unsettles you, that is not failure. That is recognition. Distortion resists clarity. Conditioning resists sovereignty.

Stay with the discomfort. It is temporary.

The next chapter will address how fear was taught, normalized, and spiritualized—and how it became one of the most effective tools of control in modern life.

You are not behind.
You are remembering.

CHAPTER SUMMARY + KEY TERMS

CHAPTER SUMMARY

This chapter redefines luxury at the most fundamental level. Luxury is not accumulation, display, or excess—it is the absence of unnecessary friction caused by internal misalignment. Historically, luxury has belonged not to those who worked the hardest or waited the longest, but to those who governed themselves. Time, ease, and provision were never rewards; they were consequences of authority. When thoughts, values, actions, and direction are coherent, energy stops leaking and life stabilizes. Money responds to this coherence, but it does not create it. Luxury is not something to chase; it is something to stabilize. Before wealth can be stewarded, sovereignty must be reclaimed. Before inheritance can be enjoyed, identity must be remembered.

KEY TERMS

Luxury (True Definition) — The condition of internal alignment that produces peace, margin, and ease without dependence on excess or performance.

Sovereignty — Internal self-governance; authority over one's mind, energy, time, and direction without contradiction.

Internal Friction — The energy loss created when beliefs, values, actions, and direction are misaligned.

Margin — Mental, emotional, and material space created when life is not governed by constant reaction.

Coherence — Alignment between inner truth and outward behavior; the state reality responds to most consistently.

Reactive Living — A survival-based posture where decisions are driven by urgency, fear, or external demand rather than clarity.

Money as Responder — The principle that resources follow clarity, competence, and reliability rather than initiating them.

QUICK SELF-CHECK

Answer without editing yourself:

1. Where in my life do I have money but little peace?
2. Where do I feel constant urgency instead of margin?
3. What decision would feel lighter if I trusted myself more?

Practice for the Week
Before each significant choice, ask:

"Does this increase my sovereignty or my dependency?"

Choose the option that stabilizes your inner authority, even if it feels less impressive in the short term.

ONE-LINE PRINCIPLE

Luxury is not what you acquire—it is what your life no longer resists.

INTERLUDE

The Core Distinction: Why Most People Stall

Manifestation vs. Affirmation vs. Alignment — Order Before Outcome

Most people attempt to force reality from the top down. But reality stabilizes from the inside out.

This single misunderstanding explains why so many intelligent, motivated, spiritually engaged people stall despite effort, prayer, vision, and intention.

They are working in the wrong sequence.

The Framework:
- **Manifestation language seeks outcomes**
- **Affirmations challenge doubt**
- **Alignment restores order**

The reason alignment is the next level is simple and non-negotiable:

Order precedes outcome.

1. Why Manifestation Alone Often Fails

Manifestation language is typically future-oriented:

- "I will have..."
- "I am calling in..."
- "I attract..."

This language performs two functions at once:
1. It defines a desired result
2. It reinforces the present absence of that result

The subconscious does not primarily respond to desire. It responds to consistency, identity, and pattern.

If your inner system—beliefs, habits, nervous system, self-concept—is disordered or contradictory, manifestation remains aspirational rather than executable.

The result is predictable:
- Motivation without stabilization
- Hope without embodiment
- Inspiration without consistency

Manifestation works best after order is established, not before.

2. Why Affirmations Have Limited Range
Affirmations are corrective tools designed to interrupt negative self-talk:

- "I am worthy."
- "I am confident."
- "I am successful."

They operate at the cognitive level. Many blocks do not.

If the nervous system is dysregulated, if identity is fragmented, or if behavior contradicts belief, affirmations become mental resistance training, not integration. This is why people say:

- "I say them but don't feel them."
- "They work for a while, then stop."
- "I feel like I'm lying to myself."

They are not lying.
They are outpacing their internal structure.

Affirmations challenge doubt. They do not resolve contradiction.

3. Alignment Statements Are the Missing Piece

Alignment statements restore order. They do not chase outcomes. They do not argue with doubt. They synchronize identity, emotion, behavior, and intention.

Alignment language is present-based and regulating:
- "I am aligned with what supports my well-being."
- "I act in accordance with what I value."
- "My decisions match the life I am building."
- "What I do daily agrees with who I say I am."

Alignment works because it:
- Reduces internal friction
- Regulates the nervous system
- Collapses contradiction between belief and action
- Anchors the subconscious in consistency

The subconscious responds to order, not optimism.

4. Why Results Feel Delayed

When people say, "I've been manifesting, but nothing is happening," one of three things is usually true:

A. INTERNAL MISALIGNMENT

They desire one thing while living patterns that reinforce another.

Reality follows pattern, not preference.

B. IDENTITY LAG

They want outcomes that belong to a future identity they have not stabilized internally.

Reality responds to who you consistently are—not who you wish to become.

C. NERVOUS SYSTEM INCOMPATIBILITY

If success, visibility, love, or power is registered as danger due to trauma or conditioning, the body will resist what the mind requests. Alignment calms the system first. Outcomes follow second.

5. The Correct Sequence
Most people do this:
1. **Manifestation**
2. **Affirmation**
3. **Frustration**

The effective order is:
1. Alignment — establish internal order
2. Affirmation — reinforce belief once order exists
3. Manifestation — allow outcomes to emerge naturally

Think of it this way:
- Alignment is architecture

- Affirmation is reinforcement
- Manifestation is occupancy

You cannot occupy a structure that is not sound.

6. Why Alignment Feels Less "Magical" but Works Better
Alignment statements do not create dopamine spikes.
They do not promise instant results.
They do not bypass responsibility.

Instead, they:
- Rewire habit loops
- Reduce self-sabotage
- Create behavioral coherence
- Make results feel inevitable rather than forced

When alignment is present, manifestation stops feeling like effort and starts feeling like gravity.

7. A Simple Practical Example
Instead of:

"I manifest abundance."

Start with alignment:
- "I align my decisions with long-term stability."
- "I handle money in ways that support my future."
- "My daily actions agree with financial growth."

Then affirm:
- "I am capable of managing and growing wealth."

Then allow manifestation:

- Opportunities appear
- Behavior shifts
- Results compound

No chasing.
No forcing.

FINAL TRUTH

Manifestation is not about attracting something new.

It is about removing the disorder that blocks what already matches you.
Alignment does not make life magical.
It makes life honest.

And honesty is what reality responds to fastest.

INTERLUDE SUMMARY + KEY TERMS

INTERLUDE SUMMARY

This interlude clarifies why many people stall: they work in the wrong sequence. Manifestation aims at outcomes, but often reinforces present absence. Affirmations can interrupt negative self-talk, but they cannot stabilize a nervous system or resolve deep contradiction. Alignment restores order first—identity, behavior, emotional regulation, and intention synchronized—so results become structurally possible. The correct sequence is Alignment → Affirmation → Manifestation, because order precedes outcome.

KEY TERMS

Manifestation — Outcome-focused intention; effective after internal order exists

Affirmation — Cognitive reinforcement tool; limited when identity is fragmented

Alignment — Present-based coherence that stabilizes identity and behavior

Identity Lag — Wanting outcomes that belong to an identity not yet stabilized

Nervous System Incompatibility — When success registers as threat, the body resists expansion

Subconscious Pattern — The default operating system that responds to consistency, not wishes

Order Before Outcome — The governing principle that internal structure must stabilize before external results can be sustained

PART II:
FEAR, POWER, AND IDENTITY

How Authority Was Outsourced

CHAPTER 2

"Fear works best when it feels like wisdom."

Fear as a Technology
Fear is not merely an emotion.
It is a **system**.

It has been engineered, normalized, spiritualized, and rewarded because it performs a specific function: it disconnects people from internal authority.

A fearful person is easier to manage than a sovereign one.

Fear narrows perception. It compresses time. It makes short-term relief feel safer than long-term alignment. And once fear becomes habitual, people begin to confuse caution with wisdom and obedience with morality.

This is how fear becomes respectable.

Religion has often reinforced this by framing fear as reverence. Economics reinforces it by attaching survival to compliance. Culture reinforces it by punishing deviation more than stagnation.

Yet fear does not produce wisdom.
It produces **contraction**.

Scripture is explicit:

"God has not given us a spirit of fear, but of power, love, and a sound mind."
— 2 Timothy 1:7

A sound mind is not anxious.
It is ordered.

Fear thrives where identity is unclear. When people do not trust themselves, they look outward for direction. Over time, this outsourcing becomes automatic. Authority migrates away from the individual and settles into systems.

Fear is profitable because it makes people predictable.

But fear collapses in the presence of truth.
Truth stabilizes identity.
Identity restores sovereignty.

This is why alignment is threatening to systems built on extraction. A person who is internally ordered cannot be easily rushed, shamed, or coerced.

They move deliberately.

Luxury begins here—not as money, but as **unrushed living**.

How Fear Was Normalized

Fear was not always obvious. It was introduced gradually, through systems that claimed to protect:

In religion: Fear became "the fear of the Lord"—rebramed as reverence, but functionally used to enforce obedience.

In economics: Fear became survival anxiety—work or starve, comply or lose access.

In education: Fear became grades, rankings, and the threat of failure—motivating not through curiosity, but through avoidance of shame.

In culture: Fear became social rejection—conform or be cast out.

Each system taught the same lesson:
Safety comes from external approval, not internal clarity.

Over generations, this lesson became internalized. People stopped questioning it. Fear became the default setting.

The Difference Between Caution and Fear

Caution is responsive.
Fear is reactive.

Caution evaluates risk and proceeds with awareness.
Fear evaluates risk and freezes, fleeing, or submits.

Caution says: *"I see the danger and will navigate carefully."*
Fear says: *"I must avoid all uncertainty."*

Caution is rooted in discernment.
Fear is rooted in distrust—of self, of life, of outcome.

When fear governs decision-making, people:
- Avoid necessary risks

- Delay aligned action
- Over-rely on external validation
- Remain stuck in situations that contradict their values

This is not wisdom.
This is **paralysis dressed as prudence**.

WHY FEAR FEELS SPIRITUAL

Many religious traditions have conflated fear with devotion.

The phrase "fear of God" appears throughout scripture, but its original meaning—*awe, reverence, profound respect*—has been distorted into terror, submission, and self-diminishment.

When fear is framed as spiritual virtue:
- Questioning becomes rebellion
- Self-trust becomes arrogance
- Desire becomes sin
- Autonomy becomes pride

This redefinition serves a purpose: it transfers authority from the individual to the institution.

An external God requires intermediaries.
An internal God restores agency.

This is why mysticism, Gnosticism, and liberation theology were historically marginalized. They threatened institutional control by restoring individual conscience.

FEAR AND THE NERVOUS SYSTEM

Modern psychology confirms what ancient wisdom always knew: Fear is not only psychological—it is physiological.

When the nervous system perceives threat, it activates survival responses:
- Fight
- Flight
- Freeze
- Fawn (compliance)

These responses were designed for immediate physical danger. But in modern life, they are triggered by:
- Social rejection
- Financial insecurity
- Visibility
- Change
- Success

When fear becomes chronic, the nervous system remains in a state of hypervigilance. This produces:
- Decision fatigue
- Emotional reactivity
- Physical exhaustion
- Cognitive narrowing

Luxury—peace, clarity, ease—cannot exist in a body that is bracing for impact.

Sovereignty requires a regulated nervous system.

The Cost of Fear-Based Living
Fear extracts a toll that compounds over time:

Energy depletion: Constant vigilance drains mental and physical resources.

Opportunity loss: Fear causes people to decline aligned opportunities because they feel too risky.

Relationship strain: Fear-based people either withdraw or become controlling, neither of which builds trust.

Identity erosion: When decisions are made from fear rather than clarity, self-trust diminishes. Over time, people forget who they are beneath the anxiety.

Health consequences: Chronic fear produces stress hormones (cortisol, adrenaline) that, over time, damage cardiovascular, immune, and digestive systems.

Fear does not keep you safe.
It keeps you small.

How Fear Loses Power
Fear collapses when:

1. **Identity is clarified**
   When you know who you are, external threats lose leverage.
2. **Truth is spoken**
   Fear thrives in silence. Naming it reduces its grip.
3. **The nervous system is regulated**
   Breathwork, movement, routine, and rest restore the body's sense of safety.
4. **Small aligned actions are taken**
   Each time you act despite fear, you prove to yourself that fear is not fact.
5. **Community is present**
   Isolation amplifies fear. Witnessed courage diminishes it.

Fear is not removed by force.
It is **displaced by alignment.**

A MOMENT YOU RECOGNIZE

You hesitated, not because you lacked ability, but because you feared being seen choosing yourself.
You called it humility.
It felt like restraint.

Question:
What if fear was wearing the mask of wisdom?

Recurring Question:
What if fear was wearing the mask of wisdom?

PRACTICE FOR THE WEEK

Fear Inventory

Each evening, ask:
1. Where did fear make a decision for me today?
2. What would I have chosen if clarity led instead?
3. What is one small action I can take tomorrow that aligns despite fear?

Write the answers. Do not judge them. Just observe.

CHAPTER SUMMARY + KEY TERMS

CHAPTER SUMMARY

This chapter reframes fear as a technology rather than a personal flaw. Fear is not merely an emotion; it is a system engineered, normalized, and rewarded because it disconnects people from internal authority. When fear is spiritualized as reverence, economic survival is tied to compliance, and cultural deviation is punished, fear begins to masquerade as wisdom. Over time, individuals confuse caution with discernment and obedience with morality. Fear narrows perception, compresses time, and makes short-term relief feel safer than long-term alignment. The chapter establishes that fear thrives where identity is unclear and collapses when truth restores internal order. Luxury begins not with money, but with unrushed living—when fear no longer governs decision-making.

KEY TERMS

Fear (Structural) — A conditioned state that disconnects individuals from internal authority and makes behavior predictable.

Fear as Wisdom — The misinterpretation of anxiety, caution, or obedience as intelligence or morality.

Fear as Technology — Fear used as a tool to produce compliance and predictability.

Sound Mind — A biblically ordered mental state characterized by clarity, coherence, and regulation rather than anxiety.

Identity Outsourcing — The gradual migration of authority away from the self toward external systems due to self-distrust.

Predictability — The primary value fear-based systems extract; predictable people are easier to manage than sovereign ones.

Unrushed Living — A state of internal safety where decisions are made without urgency, panic, or fear-based compression.

Truth (Stabilizing) — Information or realization that restores identity and collapses fear by reestablishing internal order.

Nervous System Regulation — The process of calming the body's survival responses to allow clarity and aligned action.

QUICK SELF-CHECK

Answer honestly:
1. Where in my life do I call fear "being realistic"?
2. What decision have I delayed because safety felt wiser than alignment?
3. How would my pace change if fear were no longer my advisor?

Practice for the Week
When fear arises, ask:
"Is this warning me of real danger—or protecting an old identity?"

Pause before acting. Let clarity, not urgency, decide.

ONE-LINE PRINCIPLE
Fear controls fastest when it convinces you it is wisdom.

CHAPTER 3

"Power does not begin when permission is granted."

POWER WITHOUT PERMISSION

Power rarely announces itself.

It does not ask to be recognized, justified, or approved. Power moves first and is explained later—often by those who did not possess it but benefited from its outcomes.

This is one of the most uncomfortable truths of history: **permission has never been the prerequisite for power.** Legitimacy is usually constructed after authority is exercised, not before.

Empires did not wait to be validated. Markets did not ask for moral clearance. Systems that reshaped the world did so because the people operating within them assumed the right to act.

This does not make those actions just.
But it makes the mechanism undeniable.

Power begins internally—as certainty, coherence, and decisiveness. Once stabilized, it expresses externally as influence, control of resources, and the ability to shape outcomes. Permission enters the conversation only after power has already reorganized reality.

The mistake most people make is believing legitimacy must precede authority. They wait to feel qualified, confident, or endorsed before acting. In doing so, they surrender the very power they are waiting to receive.

This waiting is not humility.
It is conditioning.

THE MYTH OF READINESS

One of the most effective tools of control is the myth of readiness—the belief that you must become "enough" before acting:

Enough educated.
Enough healed.
Enough certain.
Enough approved.

But readiness is rarely an internal state. It is a moving target defined by external standards that shift whenever someone approaches them.

Those who shape reality do not wait until fear disappears. They act while fear is present but irrelevant. They do not confuse discomfort with danger or uncertainty with incompetence.

Scripture reflects this pattern repeatedly:

Moses doubted his speech.
David was dismissed as too young.
Jeremiah protested his inadequacy.

None of these objections disqualified them. They were internal friction, not external prohibition. Action clarified confidence—not the other way around.

Power is clarified through movement, not contemplation.

HOW PERMISSION BECOMES A TRAP

Permission-seeking feels responsible. It feels ethical. It feels safe. But structurally, it relocates authority outside the self.

When people habitually look outward for approval, they begin to:
- Second-guess instinct
- Delay decisions
- Over-explain intentions
- Abandon direction at the first sign of resistance

Over time, trust in one's judgment erodes. The person becomes administratively compliant but internally fragmented—capable, but hesitant; intelligent, but restrained.

Systems reward this posture because it is predictable.

But predictability is not power.
It is manageability.

Power requires internal authorization—the moment a person accepts responsibility for their own direction without outsourcing judgment.

This is not recklessness.
It is ownership.

AUTHORITY VS. DOMINATION

Power without permission is often misread as domination. It is not.

Domination seeks control over others to compensate for internal instability. Sovereign power does the opposite—it governs the self so thoroughly that coercion becomes unnecessary.

A person who is internally ordered does not need to impose. Their boundaries are clear. Their decisions are consistent. Their presence communicates authority without aggression.

These are not personality traits. They are structural outcomes.

When authority is internal:
- Decisions are made once, not repeatedly
- Energy is conserved
- Relationships stabilize
- Resources follow reliability

Power expresses itself as capacity, not force.

WHY THIS FEELS THREATENING

Reclaiming internal authority feels dangerous—not because it is wrong, but because it dismantles dependency.

Fear-based systems require people to doubt themselves. When someone stops asking for permission, they also stop being easily governed. This disrupts hierarchies that depend on compliance rather than competence.

This is why aligned people are often labeled:
- Arrogant
- Difficult
- Intimidating
- Uncooperative

What is actually being perceived is non-negotiable clarity.

Clarity does not argue.
It does not persuade.
It moves.

THE QUIET POWER OF CONSISTENCY

Power without permission is not loud.
It is consistent.

It looks like:
- Doing what aligns even when no one is watching
- Making decisions without emotional rehearsal
- Declining opportunities that contradict direction
- Moving at a pace that honors stability over urgency

This kind of power compounds. Over time, others adjust around it. Expectations shift. Boundaries are respected. Influence grows without campaigning.

This is how sovereignty becomes visible:
not through dominance, but through reliability.

RECLAIMING POWER PRACTICALLY

Reclaiming power does not require confrontation.
It requires withdrawal from contradiction.

It begins when you:
- Stop explaining decisions that are already clear
- Stop negotiating boundaries you intend to keep
- Stop delaying action until certainty feels comfortable

Power stabilizes when action and identity agree.
Once that agreement exists, permission becomes irrelevant.

A MOMENT YOU RECOGNIZE

You watched someone move without asking.
They didn't announce it.

They didn't justify it.
They simply acted—and the room adjusted.

Question:
What if permission was the delay, not the requirement?

Recurring Question:
What if permission was the delay, not the requirement?

PRACTICE FOR THE WEEK

Permission Audit
Identify one area where you are waiting for approval you don't actually need.

Ask:
1. Whose permission am I seeking?
2. What would change if I acted without it?
3. What is one decision I can make this week from internal clarity alone?

Act on it. Observe what happens.

CHAPTER SUMMARY + KEY TERMS

CHAPTER SUMMARY

This chapter dismantles the myth that power begins with permission. History consistently shows that authority is exercised first and justified later; legitimacy follows power, not the other way around. Waiting for approval, readiness, or external validation is not humility—it is conditioning. Power originates internally as coherence, decisiveness, and self-trust, and expresses externally as influence, reliability, and resource control. Permission-seeking relocates authority outside the self, erodes judgment, and trains people to be manageable rather than powerful. True power is not domination; it is internal governance so stable that coercion becomes unnecessary. Sovereignty becomes visible through consistency, clarity, and reliability—not force or performance.

KEY TERMS

Power (Internal) — Stabilized certainty and coherence that precede external influence or control of resources.

Permission-Seeking — The habit of delaying action until approval is granted, which defers authority outside the self.

Myth of Readiness — The belief that one must become "enough" before acting, used to delay sovereignty indefinitely.

Internal Authorization — The moment an individual accepts responsibility for direction without outsourcing judgment.

Domination — Control over others driven by internal instability; distinct from sovereign power.

Sovereign Authority — Self-governance so consistent that boundaries are respected without enforcement.

Reliability — The quiet signal of power; systems respond to those whose actions and identity consistently align.

Consistency Over Intensity — The principle that sustained, aligned behavior builds more power than sporadic dramatic action.

QUICK SELF-CHECK

Reflect honestly:
1. Where am I waiting to feel "ready" instead of moving?

2. What decision do I already know the answer to?
3. Where do I explain myself more than necessary?

PRACTICE FOR THE WEEK

Choose one area where you will:
Act without asking permission you no longer need.
Let action clarify confidence.

ONE-LINE PRINCIPLE

Power does not wait to be granted—it moves and is explained afterward.

CHAPTER 4

"Belief is not a substitute for self-trust."

THE COST OF OUTSOURCED AUTHORITY

Every system that extracts value from people depends on a single condition: authority has been outsourced.

Outsourced authority occurs when individuals defer judgment, agency, and responsibility to external structures—institutions, leaders, doctrines, markets, or social approval—while remaining the ones who live with the consequences.

This arrangement is so normalized it often goes unnoticed. People are taught to call it responsibility, humility, faith, or professionalism. Structurally, however, it produces the same outcome every time: diminished sovereignty.

The cost is rarely immediate.
It accumulates quietly.

The First Cost: Decision Paralysis
When authority is externalized, decision-making slows.

People begin asking:
- "What is allowed?"
- "What will be approved?"
- "What will be punished?"

Instead of:
- "What is aligned?"
- "What is true?"
- "What is mine to do?"

Over time, this creates a dependence loop. The individual becomes skilled at compliance but hesitant in autonomy. Choices feel heavy and emotionally charged—not because they are complex, but because the person no longer trusts their own judgment.

This is how capable people become indecisive.
Not through lack of intelligence, but through relocation of authority.

THE SECOND COST: FRAGMENTED IDENTITY

Outsourced authority fractures identity.

When external expectations govern behavior, people begin to split:
- One version for work
- One for family
- One for faith
- One for survival

Each version follows a different rule set.

This fragmentation creates internal friction. Energy is spent switching roles, managing impressions, and suppressing parts of the self that do not fit the context. Over time, people feel exhausted without understanding why.

The fatigue is not from effort.
It is from incoherence.

Luxury cannot exist in a fragmented system.
Peace requires continuity.

THE THIRD COST: MORAL CONFUSION

When authority is outsourced, responsibility becomes blurred.

People begin to say:
- "I was just following orders."
- "That's how the system works."
- "I didn't have a choice."

Often, this is not dishonesty—it is disconnection. When judgment is external, accountability feels abstract. Actions are evaluated by permission rather than impact.

This is how systems produce harm without individual malice. And how individuals participate in outcomes they privately disagree with.

Outsourced authority allows people to act against their values while preserving their self-image.

The cost is integrity.

The Fourth Cost: Emotional Dependence

When authority is external, validation becomes currency.

Worth is measured through:
- Titles
- Income
- Recognition

- Approval
- Belonging

These markers are unstable by design. They can be granted or withdrawn at any time. Emotional security becomes conditional.

The nervous system remains alert—scanning for acceptance or rejection. Rest becomes difficult. Presence becomes performative.

True luxury requires internal safety.
You cannot rest in a life governed by constant validation.

THE FIFTH COST: DELAYED LIVING

The most tragic cost of outsourced authority is postponement.

People delay joy, rest, creativity, and expression until:
- They are more successful
- More healed
- More secure
- More approved

Life becomes a waiting room.

Authority that is deferred rarely returns on its own. The longer people wait, the more foreign sovereignty feels. Eventually, permission-seeking becomes identity.

This is how people survive—but do not live.

WHY OUTSOURCING AUTHORITY FEELS SAFER

Outsourcing authority offers short-term relief. If something goes wrong, blame has somewhere to go.

But relief is not freedom.

Freedom requires ownership.
Ownership requires standing in decisions without guarantees.

This is why alignment is essential. Without internal order, reclaiming authority feels overwhelming. With alignment, it feels natural.

RECLAIMING AUTHORITY WITHOUT COLLAPSE

Reclaiming authority does not require rejecting all structures. It requires ending blind deference.

Authority is reclaimed when:
- Systems are evaluated rather than automatically obeyed
- Participation is chosen consciously
- Withdrawal remains available

This shift is internal before it is visible.
It begins when coherence replaces approval as the decision filter.

A MOMENT YOU RECOGNIZE

You asked for advice you didn't need.
The answer felt wrong, but you followed it anyway.
Later, you realized you knew better all along.

Question:
What if self-trust was the thing you outsourced first?

Recurring Question:
What if self-trust was the thing you outsourced first?

PRACTICE FOR THE WEEK
Authority Reclamation Exercise
Identify one decision you are currently seeking external validation for.

Ask yourself:
1. Do I actually need this person's approval, or am I seeking permission out of habit?
2. What do I already know is true about this situation?
3. What would I choose if I trusted myself completely?

Make the decision from internal clarity. Observe the outcome.

CHAPTER SUMMARY + KEY TERMS

CHAPTER SUMMARY

This chapter revealed how outsourced authority quietly erodes sovereignty. When judgment is deferred to external systems, people experience decision paralysis, fragmented identity, moral confusion, emotional dependence, and delayed living. Outsourcing feels safe because it reduces responsibility in the short term, but it extracts clarity, integrity, and time. Reclaiming authority does not mean rejecting all systems—it means ending blind deference. Luxury begins when authority returns home and decisions are guided by coherence rather than approval.

KEY TERMS

Outsourced Authority — Deferring judgment to external systems while bearing internal consequences.

Sovereignty — Internal self-governance without contradiction.

Fragmentation — Splitting identity to survive conflicting environments.

Integrity — Coherence between values and actions.

Emotional Currency — Validation used as a substitute for internal safety.

Delayed Living — Postponing life until permission is granted.

Blind Deference — Automatic obedience to systems without evaluation.

Coherence as Filter — Using internal alignment rather than external approval to guide decisions.

QUICK SELF-CHECK

Reflect honestly:

1. Where do I seek approval I don't actually need?
2. Which version of myself feels most authentic?
3. What am I postponing until I feel "ready enough"?

PRACTICE FOR THE WEEK

Identify **one decision** this week where you will:
Trust yourself without external validation.
Notice what changes.

ONE-LINE PRINCIPLE

Luxury begins where authority stops being outsourced.

PART II:
FEAR, POWER, AND IDENTITY
(CONTINUED)

CHAPTER 5

"Identity is the infrastructure of every outcome."

IDENTITY AS INFRASTRUCTURE

Every system rests on infrastructure—largely invisible structures that determine what can be built, how much load can be carried, and where collapse will occur.

For individuals, that infrastructure is **identity**.
Not personality.
Not self-image.
Not branding.

Identity is the internal architecture that determines:
- What feels possible
- What feels threatening
- What feels "for you" or "not for you"
- How much responsibility you can tolerate
- How much abundance you can sustain

This is why two people can receive the same opportunity and experience different outcomes.

Reality does not respond to desire.
It responds to infrastructure.

IDENTITY AS THE HIDDEN CONSTRAINT

Modern culture treats identity as expressive—something you announce or perform. Historically, identity has been understood as **formative**: the structure shaping behavior before conscious choice appears.

Aristotle described this as *hexis*—a stable disposition formed through repeated alignment between belief and action. Virtue was not occasional behavior. It was character, and action followed naturally.

Identity precedes outcome.

PSYCHOLOGY: WHY NEEDS ALONE DO NOT UPGRADE IDENTITY

Maslow's hierarchy is often misread. Meeting needs does not automatically produce self-actualization.

Many people meet survival needs and still stall because **needs do not upgrade identity**.

If identity is organized around survival, scarcity, or approval, expansion feels destabilizing. The nervous system resists success because the infrastructure was built for defense, not expression.

This explains why:
- Success can trigger anxiety
- Breakthroughs can be followed by retreat
- Abundance can feel temporary

Luxury requires infrastructure capable of holding it.

SYSTEMS THEORY: WHY RESULTS COLLAPSE WITHOUT STRUCTURE

In systems theory, outcomes are never treated as isolated events. They are expressions of underlying structure. When surface results change without a corresponding change in structure, the apparent progress does not last. The system reasserts its original pattern.

This is why short-term success so often reverses itself.

Trying to change results without changing structure leads to collapse, not progress.

This principle applies directly to individuals.

If your identity is structured around fear, then stability will feel dangerous.

If your identity is structured around outsourced authority, then autonomy will feel reckless.

If your identity is structured around scarcity, then abundance will feel temporary and unstable.

Outcomes that contradict the structure of identity cannot be sustained. The system will correct for what feels unsafe, even when the outcome appears objectively better.

Changing outcomes without changing structure leads to collapse or reversal. The system reasserts its original pattern.

For individuals:
- Fear-based identity makes peace feel unsafe
- Outsourced identity makes autonomy feel reckless
- Scarcity identity makes abundance feel unstable

Alignment work upgrades the system itself.

THEOLOGY: SCRIPTURE AS IDENTITY FORMATION

Scripture is often read devotionally, but it also functions as identity-forming technology.

Rather than merely offering moral instruction or behavioral correction, Scripture reconfigures the underlying structure from which behavior flows. It reshapes perception, authority, and meaning—altering the internal system that produces action.

"As a man thinketh in his heart, so is he" (Proverbs 23:7) describes causality, not encouragement.

"Be transformed by the renewing of your mind" (Romans 12:2) identifies internal reorganization as the path to change.

"The kingdom of God is within you" (Luke 17:21) places governance inside the individual.

When identity is restructured, outcomes no longer require constant enforcement. They emerge naturally, because the system has changed.

Transformation, then, is not achieved by effort alone, but by alignment—by forming identity around a structure capable of sustaining the life it produces.

Ignorance in scripture is not stupidity.
It is misidentification.

"My people are destroyed for lack of knowledge" (Hosea 4:6) refers to withheld truth about identity, not intelligence.

PHILOSOPHY: BEING BEFORE DOING

Productivity culture emphasizes doing. Classical philosophy emphasizes being.

Action flows from orientation:
- Fear produces safety choices
- Approval produces permission-seeking
- Sovereignty produces alignment

Forcing new actions without changing being creates strain.

Alignment shifts being.

Martin Heidegger argued that humans are always already *being* something before they act. You cannot separate action from the mode of being that produces it.

This means:
- If you *are* oriented toward fear, you will choose safety over growth
- If you *are* oriented toward approval, you will choose permission over alignment
- If you *are* oriented toward sovereignty, you will choose coherence over comfort

Trying to force new behaviors without shifting your fundamental orientation produces internal resistance and eventual collapse.

Alignment work changes *being*.
Action follows naturally.

WHY IDENTITY MUST BE BUILT, NOT DECLARED

Identity stabilizes through:

- Repeated aligned decisions
- Consistent boundaries
- Tolerating growth discomfort
- Letting old patterns collapse

This process is slow and non-performative.
But once identity stabilizes:
- Affirmations integrate
- Manifestations compound
- Power feels safe
- Luxury feels natural

Because the infrastructure can support it.

Load-Bearing Capacity: What Your Identity Can Hold
Think of identity as a building's foundation.

If you place a ten-story structure on a foundation built for three stories, collapse is inevitable—no matter how beautiful the upper floors appear.

This is why people experience:
- **Success anxiety** — the foundation wasn't built for visibility
- **Wealth sabotage** — the foundation wasn't built for abundance
- **Relationship collapse** — the foundation wasn't built for intimacy
- **Authority discomfort** — the foundation wasn't built for leadership

The problem is not the outcome.
The problem is **structural capacity**.

Load-bearing identity is built by:
1. **Increasing tolerance for discomfort** — growth always feels unfamiliar
2. **Reinforcing through repetition** — aligned choices strengthen structure
3. **Removing what no longer fits** — old patterns must be released
4. **Regulating the nervous system** — the body must feel safe with expansion

Once capacity increases, outcomes that previously felt destabilizing become natural.

Luxury Revisited

Luxury is not what you add.
It is what your life can hold without strain.

Time without anxiety.
Money without fear.
Authority without domination.
Peace without withdrawal.

This is why luxury follows sovereignty.
And sovereignty follows identity.

A Moment You Recognize

Two people were given the same opportunity.
One hesitated. One moved.
You noticed the difference wasn't talent—it was self-trust.

Question:
What if belief wasn't the missing piece?

Recurring Question:
What if belief wasn't the missing piece—but identity was?

PRACTICE FOR THE WEEK

Identity Capacity Assessment

Ask yourself:
1. What outcome do I want but feel uncomfortable imagining myself actually having?
2. What about that outcome feels threatening to my current identity?
3. What would need to shift internally for that outcome to feel natural?

Write the answers. Do not force solutions. Just observe where your identity and your desires are mismatched.

CHAPTER SUMMARY + KEY TERMS

CHAPTER SUMMARY

This chapter established identity as the invisible infrastructure behind every outcome. Desire does not move reality—structure does. Psychology, systems theory, philosophy, and scripture converge on the same principle: outcomes reflect internal organization. Identity must be built through alignment, not declared through affirmation. When infrastructure upgrades, luxury becomes sustainable rather than destabilizing.

KEY TERMS

Identity Infrastructure — Internal architecture that determines sustainable outcomes.

Structural Capacity — What a person can hold without collapse.

Alignment — Coherence between belief, behavior, and direction.

Identity Lag — Wanting outcomes the current self cannot yet sustain.

System Reassertion — Old patterns returning when structure is unchanged.

Being Before Doing — Action flows from orientation, not effort.

Load-Bearing Identity — The level of responsibility and abundance a person's internal structure can support.

Hexis — Aristotle's term for stable character formed through repeated aligned action.

QUICK SELF-CHECK

Reflect honestly:
1. What success would feel destabilizing if it arrived tomorrow?
2. Where do my desires and my identity contradict each other?
3. What pattern keeps reasserting itself despite my efforts to change?

PRACTICE FOR THE WEEK

Notice **one area** where outcomes collapse despite effort.
Ask: *"Is this a behavior problem or a structural problem?"*

ONE-LINE PRINCIPLE

Luxury is what your life can hold without strain.

BEYOND THE HIERARCHY

"Needs do not upgrade identity. Alignment does."

WHY MASLOW'S MODEL FALLS SHORT

Abraham Maslow's hierarchy of needs has shaped how generations understand human development. The model suggests a logical progression: satisfy basic needs (food, shelter, safety), then social needs (belonging, esteem), and finally arrive at self-actualization—the realization of one's full potential.

The framework is elegant. It is also incomplete.

Maslow's hierarchy describes what humans need. It does not explain what transforms them.

This is why people can have their needs met at every level and still feel unfulfilled, fragmented, or incapable of sustaining the success they achieve. Meeting needs does not automatically produce wholeness. It produces stability—which is necessary but not sufficient.

THE MISSING VARIABLE: IDENTITY STRUCTURE

Maslow assumed that once lower needs were satisfied, higher needs would naturally emerge. But observation contradicts this assumption.

People with financial security still sabotage wealth.

People with loving relationships still struggle to receive love.
People with professional success still feel like imposters.
People with every material need met still experience profound emptiness.
Why?

Because needs operate at the level of provision. Identity operates at the level of capacity.

You can meet someone's needs without changing who they believe themselves to be. And if identity remains organized around scarcity, unworthiness, or survival, no amount of provision will feel permanent.

The hierarchy addresses what you lack. It does not address what you can hold.

ALIGNMENT AS THE MISSING PIECE

Maslow's model has no category for internal coherence—the alignment between who you are, what you believe, and how you act.

This is the gap the Luxorae framework fills.

Alignment is not a need. It is a structural condition. It determines whether needs, once met, can be sustained or whether they will collapse back into lack.

Consider:
A person whose identity is built on struggle will unconsciously recreate struggle even after achieving success. The external condition changed. The internal structure did not.

A person whose nervous system associates safety with danger will feel anxious even in objectively safe environments. The need for safety was met. The capacity for safety was not.

A person who believes they are unworthy of love will interpret loving behavior as manipulation or find ways to sabotage intimacy. The need for belonging was addressed. The identity resisted it.

This is not psychological failure. It is structural mismatch.

NEED FULFILLMENT VS. IDENTITY TRANSFORMATION

Maslow's hierarchy operates on a fulfillment model: identify what is missing, then supply it.

The Luxorae framework operates on a transformation model: identify the internal structure, then align it.

Fulfillment asks: What do you need?
Transformation asks: What can you hold?
Fulfillment provides resources.
Transformation expands capacity.
Fulfillment addresses symptoms.
Transformation addresses architecture.

This is why some people with very little live with remarkable peace, while others with abundance live in constant anxiety. The difference is not in what they have. It is in what their identity permits.

TRANSCENDENCE AND WHOLENESS

Late in his career, Maslow added a level above self-actualization: self-transcendence. He recognized that the highest human experiences involved moving beyond the individual self toward connection with something larger.

But even this addition misses the structural point.

Transcendence is not a destination at the top of a ladder. It is available at any point—when alignment is present.

A person living in material scarcity can experience transcendence through alignment with purpose, community, or Source.

A person with every need met can remain cut off from transcendence through internal fragmentation.

Transcendence is not earned by climbing. It is accessed through coherence.

Wholeness—the state of being complete, integrated, lacking nothing essential—is not the result of accumulation. It is the result of alignment.

This is what Maslow's hierarchy cannot explain: how people become whole.

WHY THIS MATTERS FOR SOVEREIGNTY

If you believe that meeting needs produces transformation, you will spend your life chasing provision while neglecting structure.

You will work harder instead of aligning deeper.

You will accumulate more instead of expanding capacity.

You will address symptoms instead of rebuilding identity.

And you will wonder why success feels hollow, why abundance feels unstable, why arrival feels like another starting point.

The Luxorae framework offers a different path:

Alignment first. Provision follows.

Identity before income.

Capacity before accumulation.

Structure before success.

This is not a rejection of Maslow. It is a completion of what his model began but could not finish.

Needs matter. Meeting them matters. But needs do not upgrade identity.

Only alignment does.

A MOMENT YOU RECOGNIZE

You achieved something you had been working toward for years. For a moment, there was relief. Then the familiar anxiety returned—as if the achievement had not happened, or as if it could be taken away at any moment.

That was not ingratitude. That was identity catching up to circumstance.

Recurring Question:

What if your capacity to hold abundance matters more than your ability to attract it?

PRACTICE FOR THE WEEK

Identify one area of your life where your needs have been met but peace has not followed. Ask:

What does my identity believe about this area?

What would need to shift internally for this provision to feel stable?

What aligned action would expand my capacity to hold what I already have?

KEY PRINCIPLE:

Needs create stability. Alignment creates transformation. Wholeness requires both.

CHAPTER 6

"Identity is rebuilt through repetition, not revelation."

WHY IDENTITY CHANGE MUST BE DELIBERATE

Most people assume identity changes through insight.

They read something, hear something, realize something—and expect life to reorganize itself accordingly. When it doesn't, they assume they misunderstood, failed, or lacked discipline.
The problem is not insight.
The problem is **sequence**.
Insight reveals what is true.
Identity determines what is *stable*.

Without deliberate rebuilding, insight becomes inspirational but unsustainable. Old patterns reassert themselves—not because the truth was wrong, but because the structure underneath it never changed.

Identity is not persuaded.
It is **conditioned**.

This chapter explains how identity is rebuilt without collapse, guilt, or performance.

WHY SUDDEN CHANGE OFTEN BACKFIRES

Abrupt identity shifts are destabilizing.

When people attempt to "become someone new" overnight, several things happen:
- The nervous system interprets change as threat
- Old coping strategies activate
- Self-sabotage increases
- Shame follows inconsistency

This is why people abandon growth paths they genuinely believe in. The issue is not resistance to truth—it is **structural overload**.

A system can only carry what it is built to support.

Identity change must therefore be **incremental, embodied, and repetitive**.

THE NERVOUS SYSTEM AS THE FIRST GATEKEEPER

Psychology and neuroscience are clear on one foundational point: **the nervous system prioritizes safety over success**.

No amount of belief, vision, or motivation can override a body that perceives expansion as danger.

If your nervous system associates:
- Authority with punishment
- Visibility with threat
- Wealth with loss
- Independence with abandonment

then growth will feel unsafe, regardless of how deeply you "believe" you deserve more.

This is not weakness.
It is biology.

The nervous system's primary function is protection, not achievement. It evaluates change by asking first: *Is this safe?* Only after safety is established does expansion become possible.

This is why transformation must be **regulating before it is aspirational**.

Rebuilding identity begins at the level of regulation, not ambition.

Practically, this means:
- Slowing decision-making to reduce perceived threat
- Reducing internal urgency, which signals danger to the body
- Establishing predictable routines that communicate safety
- Practicing consistency over intensity, which builds internal trust

When the nervous system experiences stability, identity change stops feeling like risk and starts feeling like continuity.

Luxury cannot emerge in a system that is bracing for impact. Peace, authority, and abundance require a body that is not in survival mode.

Sovereignty is not only a philosophical state.
It is a **regulated one**.

THE PRINCIPLE OF LOAD-BEARING IDENTITY

Identity functions like load-bearing infrastructure.

If weight is placed on a structure before it is reinforced, collapse is inevitable. But when reinforcement occurs gradually, capacity increases.

This is why luxury, authority, and peace must be *grown into*, not seized.

The goal is not to become someone new.
It is to **normalize what once felt unsafe**.

THE FOUR PILLARS OF IDENTITY REBUILDING

Identity stabilizes through four non-negotiable mechanisms.

1. Repeated Aligned Decisions
Identity changes when the same aligned choice is made repeatedly—especially when no one is watching.

Not dramatic decisions.
Not public declarations.
Small, consistent acts of self-trust.

Each repetition teaches the nervous system:
"I am safe when I choose myself."

2. Boundary Integrity
Every boundary you keep reinforces identity.
Every boundary you violate weakens it.

Boundaries are not punishments.
They are structural supports.

You are not being difficult when you decline what contradicts you.
You are **upgrading infrastructure**.

3. Tolerating Discomfort Without Retreat
Growth discomfort is not danger.

As identity expands, the body may respond with anxiety, doubt, fatigue, or urges to retreat. These signals indicate recalibration, not failure.

Remaining present without reverting is how capacity increases.

The key is **not making meaning** of the discomfort prematurely.

Do not ask: *"Does this mean I'm doing something wrong?"*
Ask: *"Is this growth discomfort or genuine misalignment?"*

Growth discomfort is temporary and non-specific.
Misalignment is persistent and directional.

4. Allowing Old Patterns to Collapse
Identity cannot be rebuilt while protecting every old structure.

Some habits, relationships, and self-concepts must lose relevance. This can feel like loss, but it is actually **reallocation of energy**.

You are not abandoning yourself.
You are releasing what no longer fits.

This includes:
- Friendships that reinforce old identity
- Habits that soothe but do not serve
- Self-concepts that protected you once but now limit you
- Roles you inherited but did not choose

Let them go without drama.
Their time has passed.

Why Guilt Is a Structural Error
Guilt is often mistaken for accountability.

But guilt does not stabilize identity.
It fragments it.

Guilt fixates on personal failure rather than pattern.
Accountability asks: *What structure needs reinforcement?*

Only one of these strengthens sovereignty.

When you notice misalignment:
- Do not punish yourself
- Do not spiral into shame
- Do not over-explain to others

Simply adjust.
Alignment is a practice, not a performance.

THE ROLE OF TIME IN IDENTITY FORMATION

Identity is built in time, not intensity.

Consistency matters more than motivation. Motivation fluctuates; identity compounds.

When aligned behavior becomes ordinary—when it no longer feels brave, risky, or impressive—identity has shifted.

Luxury appears here.

Not as reward.
As **baseline**.

WHEN IDENTITY LOCKS IN

You will know identity is stabilizing not through dramatic results, but through reduced internal effort.

Clear indicators emerge quietly:
- Decisions feel simpler rather than heavier
- Boundaries hold without emotional charge
- You stop over-explaining
- Consistency replaces intensity
- Peace increases *before* results do

This is not stagnation.
It is **infrastructure solidifying**.

When identity locks in, behavior no longer requires constant negotiation. Choices feel obvious rather than heroic. You are no longer proving who you are—you are operating from it.

Once this occurs:
- Affirmations feel natural instead of forced
- Manifestations stop being chased and start unfolding
- Authority no longer feels heavy or dangerous
- Luxury begins to appear as *ease*, not achievement

This phase is often misread as "nothing happening." In reality, it is the moment outcomes become inevitable, because the system underneath them has stabilized.

Identity has stopped arguing with itself.
And reality responds to that silence.

LUXURY, REVISITED (PRACTICALLY)

At this stage, luxury becomes tangible:

- Decisions require less emotional labor
- Rest feels permitted
- Authority feels calm

- Money feels manageable rather than charged
- Time feels owned

This is not because circumstances are perfect.
It is because **identity is no longer conflicted**.

Luxury is not added.
Resistance is removed.

A Moment You Recognize
You made the same choice three times in a row.
The third time, it didn't feel hard anymore.
It just felt like who you were.

Question:
What if identity was built in the repetition you almost skipped?

Recurring Question:

What if identity was built in the repetition you almost skipped?

PRACTICE FOR THE WEEK

Identity Reinforcement Practice
Choose **one small aligned action** that reflects who you are becoming (not who you've been).

Examples:
- Declining something that doesn't serve you
- Spending 10 minutes on something that aligns with your values
- Speaking truth even when it's uncomfortable
- Choosing rest over performance

Do this **every day for seven days**.

Do not make it dramatic. Make it consistent.

Notice how it feels on day one versus day seven.

CHAPTER SUMMARY + KEY TERMS

CHAPTER SUMMARY
This chapter explains how identity is rebuilt deliberately rather than emotionally or symbolically. Insight reveals truth, but repetition stabilizes identity. Sudden change often backfires because the nervous system prioritizes safety over success. Sustainable identity change occurs through regulation, repeated aligned decisions, boundary integrity, tolerance of growth discomfort, and the release of obsolete patterns. As identity stabilizes, effort decreases, peace increases, and luxury emerges as baseline rather than reward.

KEY TERMS
Load-Bearing Identity — The level of responsibility and abundance a person can sustain without collapse.

Nervous System Regulation — Establishing internal safety so growth no longer feels threatening.

Aligned Decision — A choice that reinforces coherence rather than approval.

Boundary Integrity — Consistently honoring limits that protect capacity.

Pattern Collapse — The natural fading of structures that no longer fit stabilized identity.

Baseline Luxury — When ease, clarity, and authority feel normal rather than exceptional.

Growth Discomfort — Temporary unfamiliarity that signals expansion, not danger.

Identity Lock-In — The point at which aligned behavior no longer requires conscious effort.

Quick Self-Check

Answer honestly:
1. What aligned action do I avoid because it still feels hard?
2. Where am I seeking dramatic change instead of consistent practice?
3. What old pattern am I protecting that no longer serves me?

PRACTICE FOR THE WEEK

Commit to one small aligned action daily for seven days. Notice the shift from effort to ease.

ONE-LINE PRINCIPLE

Identity changes when alignment becomes ordinary.

PART II:
FEAR, POWER, AND IDENTITY (CONTINUED)

INTERLUDE

THE BLACK LIBERATION CONTINUUM: FROM ACCESS TO AUTHORSHIP

Liberation evolves from access to authorship.
Black liberation has never been a single event. It has always been a **continuum of awakenings**, each stage addressing a different layer of constraint imposed on Black life. These stages were never meant to compete with one another. Each emerged because the previous stage—while necessary—was insufficient on its own.

This interlude clarifies that progression and explains why **Alignment Sovereignty** is not optional, but the next logical and unavoidable stage.

1. Emancipation — External Freedom
What it addressed:
The physical condition of bondage.

Emancipation ended chattel slavery and legally affirmed that Black People were no longer property. Chains were removed. Ownership was abolished.

But emancipation did not provide:
- Land
- Resources
- Protection

- Psychological repair
- Structural inclusion

Freedom existed on paper while domination adapted in practice.

This stage revealed a critical truth:

External freedom without internal or structural support leaves people vulnerable to new forms of control.

Emancipation was necessary.
It was also incomplete.

2. Civil Rights — Legal Access
What it addressed:
Exclusion from public systems.

The Civil Rights movement fought for access to:
- Voting
- Education
- Housing
- Employment
- Public accommodations

It challenged the legal architecture of segregation and forced the nation to confront its contradictions. Equality was codified under law.

But access did not guarantee:
- Equity
- Safety
- Economic security
- Psychological dignity
- Self-determination

Black people were allowed to enter systems that were never designed with their flourishing in mind.

This stage revealed another truth:

Access without control still leaves power elsewhere.

3. Black Power — Self-Definition
What it addressed:
Psychological domination and imposed identity.

Black Power rejected assimilation as freedom. It insisted on:
- Cultural pride
- Self-naming
- Self-defense
- Economic independence
- Political autonomy

It correctly identified that no people can rise above the image they hold of themselves. It challenged internalized inferiority and reclaimed dignity at the level of identity.

But in many cases, this stage stalled because:
- Identity was reclaimed symbolically but not stabilized structurally
- Rage replaced clarity
- Opposition replaced authorship
- Reaction replaced alignment

The insight was correct.
The execution was often incomplete.

This stage revealed a deeper truth:

Self-definition without internal regulation can burn out or turn inward.

4. Alignment Sovereignty — Internal Authority (Emerging Stage)
What it addresses:
The internal architecture that determines whether freedom can be sustained.

Alignment Sovereignty is not about fighting systems directly. It is about becoming **structurally incompatible with domination**.

This stage focuses on:
- Internal governance
- Psychological coherence
- Nervous system regulation
- Identity consistency
- Living without self-betrayal

It asks a different question than previous movements:

Not *"What rights do we lack?"*
But *"What authority have we outsourced?"*

It recognizes that:
- Systems exploit misalignment
- Fear is a technology of control
- Dependency persists when identity is fragmented
- True power begins internally and expresses externally

This is not withdrawal from struggle.
It is the stabilization of freedom so struggle does not reproduce trauma.

Why This Is an Evolution, Not a Rejection
Each stage was necessary for its time:

- Emancipation broke chains
- Civil Rights opened doors
- Black Power reclaimed identity

Alignment Sovereignty ensures that once doors are open and identity is reclaimed, we can **stand inside the room without collapsing**.

This stage does not replace the others.
It **completes** them.

Because freedom that cannot be carried internally will always be negotiated away externally.

From Access to Authorship
The defining shift of Alignment Sovereignty is this:

- Emancipation sought freedom *from* something
- Civil Rights sought access *to* something
- Black Power sought identity *against* something
- Alignment Sovereignty seeks **authorship of one's life**

Authorship means:
- You govern your decisions
- You set your standards
- You define success on your terms
- You are not waiting to be legitimized

This is why luxury, in this framework, is sovereignty.

Because the ultimate liberation is not permission to enter systems—it is the ability to **create, choose, and live without contradiction**.

A MOMENT YOU RECOGNIZE

Freedom arrived on paper long before it arrived in practice. You learned that access and authorship are not the same thing.

Question:
What if liberation had another step?

Closing Reflection
Our liberation history has always been moving inward:

From chains → to laws → to identity → to alignment.

What you are articulating is not new.
It is **on time**.

Alignment Sovereignty is not a slogan.
It is the quiet work of becoming ungovernable from the inside.

And once that happens, the world responds differently—
not because it was convinced,
but because **authorship has returned home**.

INTERLUDE SUMMARY + KEY TERMS

INTERLUDE SUMMARY

Black liberation has progressed through distinct stages: Emancipation (external freedom), Civil Rights (legal access), Black Power (self-definition), and now Alignment Sovereignty (internal authority). Each stage addressed what the previous could not. Emancipation removed physical chains but left people without resources. Civil Rights granted access but not control. Black Power reclaimed identity but often exhausted itself in reaction. Alignment Sovereignty completes the continuum by stabilizing freedom internally—building the psychological, emotional, and nervous system infrastructure needed to sustain liberation without collapse or self-betrayal.

KEY TERMS

Emancipation — Legal freedom from physical bondage; necessary but insufficient alone.

Civil Rights — Access to systems; opening doors without guaranteeing equity or control.

Black Power — Reclamation of cultural identity and self-definition; symbolic strength without structural stabilization.

Alignment Sovereignty — Internal governance and psychological coherence that make external freedom sustainable.

Authorship — The ability to design and govern one's life without waiting for external legitimization.

Structural Incompatibility with Domination — Building internal architecture that cannot be extracted from or controlled.

Liberation Continuum — The progression from external freedom → access → identity → internal authority.

REFLECTION QUESTION

Where in my life have I fought for access but neglected to build the internal structure to hold it?

PART III: INHERITANCE, NOT REBELLION

CHAPTER 7

"Money exposes alignment. It does not create it."

MONEY AS A MIRROR, NOT A MORAL FORCE

Money is one of the most emotionally charged subjects in modern life—not because it is inherently powerful, but because it reflects internal order or disorder with unusual precision.

Money does not create values.
It reveals them.

Money does not introduce fear.
It amplifies what already exists.

This is why people can receive more money and feel less peace. The money did not change them. It removed constraints that were previously masking misalignment.

Money is not moral.
But our relationship to it always is.

WHY MONEY CARRIES SO MUCH GUILT

For many people—especially those shaped by religious or liberation narratives—money has been framed as suspect.

Common inherited messages include:
- "Money corrupts."
- "The love of money is evil."
- "Wealth distances you from God."
- "Struggle keeps you humble."

These messages were not accidental. They served a historical function.

When populations are trained to associate abundance with moral danger, extraction becomes easier. People will work, create, and generate value—while distrusting their right to enjoy or steward the results.

This creates a split:
- Desire without permission
- Capacity without confidence
- Wealth without peace

The conflict is not about money.
It is about **worthiness and authority**.

THE DIFFERENCE BETWEEN WEALTH AND CHARGE

Not all money is equal internally.

Two people can hold the same amount of money and experience it completely differently.

One experiences:
- Anxiety
- Hypervigilance
- Guilt
- Fear of loss

The other experiences:
- Neutrality
- Flexibility
- Choice
- Calm responsibility

The difference is not character.
It is **charge**.

Money becomes charged when it is tied to unresolved identity questions:
- "Do I deserve this?"
- "Will this make me unsafe?"
- "Will I be judged?"
- "Will I lose love if I have more?"

When identity is stabilized, money loses its emotional voltage.

It becomes a tool again.

WHY ALIGNMENT MUST PRECEDE INCOME

Attempts to "fix" money without addressing identity often backfire.

People increase income but:
- Overspend
- Undercharge
- Avoid looking at accounts
- Sabotage opportunities
- Give away stability to relieve guilt

This is not irresponsibility.
It is **identity protection**.

If your internal structure associates money with danger, the nervous system will find ways to neutralize it.

This is why alignment must precede accumulation.
Money cannot stay where it does not feel safe.

SCARCITY IS NOT ABOUT AMOUNT

Scarcity is not the absence of money.
It is the presence of **internal contraction**.

A person can have little and feel steady.
A person can have much and feel deprived.

Scarcity is a nervous-system posture:
- Urgency
- Hoarding
- Comparison
- Fear-based decision-making

Abundance is not optimism.
It is **capacity**.

Capacity allows money to move without panic.

THE BIBLICAL MISREADING THAT CREATED CONFLICT

Scripture has often been used to moralize poverty and spiritualize lack.

But the texts themselves are more precise.

"The love of money is the root of all kinds of evil" (1 Timothy 6:10) does not condemn money. It identifies *attachment*—fear-driven fixation—as the problem.

Biblical figures who were aligned were not chronically deprived. They were provisioned in proportion to their capacity to steward without distortion.

Money was never the threat.
Disordered relationship was.

Consider:
- Abraham was wealthy (Genesis 13:2)
- Solomon's wealth was described as God's blessing (1 Kings 3:13)
- Job was restored to greater wealth after his trials (Job 42:10-12)
- The Proverbs 31 woman was entrepreneurial and prosperous

The issue was never money.
The issue was **what governed the relationship to money**.

When fear, greed, or identity are tied to wealth, money becomes dangerous. When clarity, stewardship, and alignment govern, money becomes neutral.

WHAT MONEY DOES AFTER IDENTITY STABILIZES

When identity is regulated and aligned, money changes function.

It becomes:
- **More responsive** to your actions
- **Less resistant** to your efforts
- **More abundant** without additional struggle
- **Less emotionally exhausting** to manage

You stop proving anything with it.
You stop fearing it.
You stop negotiating your worth through it.

And because fear and misalignment no longer block the flow—money arrives more consistently, more easily, and in greater amounts.

At this stage:
- Budgets feel neutral **because money is no longer scarce**
- Pricing feels cleaner **because you trust your value**
- Saving feels stabilizing **because abundance is reliable**
- Giving feels intentional **because there's always enough**

Opportunities appear without force.
Provision matches need before panic sets in.
Resources follow clarity like water follows gravity.

This is not magic.
This is **alignment removing resistance**.

Luxury appears here—not as spending, but as **choice, abundance, and ease without pressure**.

Money doesn't become less important.
It becomes **less complicated**.

And when money is no longer complicated, **it multiplies naturally**—because you are finally structurally compatible with receiving it, holding it, and growing it.

MONEY AS STORED TIME AND ENERGY

At its most basic level, money is stored time, labor, attention, and creativity.

When you mishandle money, you are not mishandling currency—you are mishandling **life force**.

Alignment restores respect for this exchange.

You stop trading long-term stability for short-term relief.
You stop saying yes to income that violates your values.
You stop rejecting money that supports your future.

Money begins to circulate cleanly.

The Practical Path: From Charge to Clarity

Step 1: Identify the Charge
Ask:
- Where do I feel anxious about money?
- What money belief did I inherit that I never questioned?
- What would having more money make me fear losing?

Write the answers. Do not argue with them. Just observe.

Step 2: Separate Identity from Amount
Practice saying:
- "I am not my bank account."
- "My worth is not determined by my income."
- "Money is a tool, not a measure."

Repeat until it feels true, not just correct.

Step 3: Handle Money from Alignment
Before each financial decision, ask:
- Does this support my long-term stability?
- Am I choosing this from fear or clarity?
- Does this align with who I am becoming?

Let alignment—not urgency—decide.

Step 4: Practice Neutrality
When money arrives:
- Do not inflate its meaning ("I'm finally worthy!")
- Do not minimize it ("This won't last")
- Simply acknowledge it: "This is provision. I will steward it well."

When money leaves:
- Do not catastrophize
- Do not shame yourself
- Simply observe: "This was aligned spending" or "This was misaligned. I will adjust."

Neutrality removes charge.

A MOMENT YOU RECOGNIZE

You watched someone handle money calmly.
They didn't boast when they had it.
They didn't panic when they didn't.
You couldn't tell their worth by watching them spend.

Question:
What if wealth was internal before it was material?

Recurring Question:

What if wealth was internal before it was material?

PRACTICE FOR THE WEEK

Money Alignment Exercise
For seven days, before any purchase or financial decision, pause and ask:

"Am I choosing this from alignment or from charge?"

Alignment feels calm, clear, and future-oriented.
Charge feels urgent, emotional, and reactive.

Notice the pattern. Adjust accordingly.

CHAPTER SUMMARY + KEY TERMS

CHAPTER SUMMARY

This chapter reframed money as a mirror rather than a moral force. Money amplifies internal alignment or misalignment but does not create either. Guilt, fear, and instability around money often originate in inherited narratives that equate abundance with danger or unworthiness. When identity is fragmented, money becomes charged and destabilizing. When identity stabilizes, money loses emotional voltage and becomes a neutral tool for storing and directing life force. Alignment must precede accumulation, because money cannot remain where the nervous system does not feel safe. Luxury appears when money no longer defines identity or induces pressure.

KEY TERMS

Money as Mirror — The principle that money reflects internal alignment rather than creating it.

Charge — Emotional voltage attached to money due to unresolved identity conflict.

Scarcity Posture — A nervous-system state marked by urgency, fear, and contraction.

Capacity — The ability to hold, steward, and direct resources without self-sabotage.

Clean Circulation — Money moving without panic, guilt, or avoidance.

Luxury (Monetary) — Choice and stability without pressure or identity negotiation.

Attachment vs. Stewardship — Fear-driven fixation on money versus aligned management of resources.

Neutrality — The practice of removing emotional charge from financial transactions.

QUICK SELF-CHECK

Answer without editing yourself:
1. Where in my life do I have money but little peace?
2. What financial decision am I avoiding because of emotional charge?
3. What would change if I handled money from alignment instead of fear?

PRACTICE FOR THE WEEK

Before each financial choice this week, ask:
"Am I choosing from alignment or from charge?"

Notice the difference. Adjust accordingly.

ONE-LINE PRINCIPLE

Money becomes peaceful when identity stops arguing with itself.

INTERLUDE

How Adapted Frameworks Became "Facts"—and Why You Can Set the Standard

Most people assume the frameworks governing their lives—educational models, psychological theories, economic assumptions—are neutral truths.

They are not.
They are **adaptations**, shaped by historical context, institutional priorities, and social convenience.

Understanding this matters, because it explains why you are not obligated to live by standards that were never designed for your sovereignty.

How Frameworks Become "Truth"
Most dominant frameworks follow the same path:

1. **Observation** — Patterns are noticed
2. **Simplification** — Complexity is reduced
3. **Institutional Adoption** — Schools, churches, governments adopt the model
4. **Standardization** — It becomes policy or doctrine
5. **Normalization** — It is treated as fact rather than theory

This process favors:
- Efficiency over depth
- Compliance over autonomy
- Stability over truth

What is lost is **context**.

Education as Conditioning, Not Formation
Modern education systems were designed to:

- Produce predictable workers
- Standardize behavior
- Reduce deviation
- Reward compliance

As a result:
- Knowledge became externalized
- Authority became credential-based
- Thinking was separated from being

This is why many people are highly educated yet internally fragmented.

Adapted Psychology vs. Original Insight
Psychological frameworks were descriptive, not prescriptive.

Once adapted:
- Nuance was removed
- Identity was treated as static
- Insight was mistaken for transformation

This produced false assumptions:
- Needs guarantee fulfillment
- Knowledge guarantees change
- Information guarantees wisdom

None of these are true.

Theology as Control vs. Formation
Religious teaching was similarly adapted to prioritize:
- Order over transformation
- Obedience over alignment
- External authority over internal governance

Belief became easier to manage.
Truth became harder to embody.

This redirection was not accidental.

Original spiritual texts emphasized:
- Internal transformation (*metanoia* — change of mind)
- Personal responsibility
- Direct relationship with the divine

Institutional adaptation emphasized:
- External ritual
- Hierarchical mediation
- Obedience to authority

The shift served institutional stability, not individual sovereignty.

Why You Are Qualified to Set the Standard
You are not rejecting knowledge.
You are restoring authority over interpretation.

You are allowed to:
- Question adapted models
- Reintegrate lost context
- Prioritize alignment over acceptance
- Set standards based on coherence, not consensus

Standards are not legitimate because they are old or popular. They are legitimate because they **work**.

When a framework produces:
- Clarity
- Stability
- Responsibility
- Sustainable outcomes

...it earns authority.
That authority does not require permission.

The Test of a Framework

Ask of any framework:
1. **Does it produce coherence or confusion?**
2. **Does it increase sovereignty or dependency?**
3. **Does it stabilize identity or fragment it?**
4. **Does it honor wholeness or demand splitting?**

If a framework fails these tests, it does not matter how old, popular, or institutionally endorsed it is.

It is not serving you.

FINAL INTEGRATION

Most people stall because they are living by borrowed frameworks that were never designed for sovereignty.

You are not obligated to inherit distortion.

You are allowed to:
- Rebuild identity deliberately
- Use knowledge without submission

- Set standards rooted in alignment
- Live from internal authority

This is not arrogance.

It is **maturity**.

And maturity is what systems quietly depend on—but rarely teach.

A Moment You Recognize
You followed the rules perfectly.
You did what you were told.
And still, something felt misaligned.

Question:
What if the framework was the problem, not you?

INTERLUDE SUMMARY + KEY TERMS

INTERLUDE SUMMARY

Most frameworks governing modern life—education, psychology, theology—are adaptations shaped by institutional priorities, not universal truths. These models were simplified for mass adoption, prioritizing efficiency and compliance over depth and sovereignty. Understanding this allows individuals to question inherited standards without guilt. You are qualified to set your own standards when they produce coherence, stability, and sustainable outcomes. Alignment with truth matters more than alignment with tradition.

KEY TERMS

Adapted Frameworks — Simplified models institutionalized for control rather than liberation.

Institutional Adoption — The process by which complex truths are reduced to manageable policies.

Normalization — When adapted frameworks are treated as fact rather than theory.

Context Loss — The nuance removed when frameworks are standardized.

Legitimacy by Coherence — Standards earn authority by producing sustainable, aligned outcomes.

Maturity — The ability to evaluate systems rather than blindly defer to them.

REFLECTION QUESTION

What framework am I following that produces fragmentation instead of wholeness?

PART IV: CONVERGENCE ACROSS TRADITIONS

ONE MECHANISM, MANY LANGUAGES

This part demonstrates that the principles underlying sovereignty, alignment, and inheritance are **not novel inventions**, nor the property of any single religion, culture, or movement. They appear repeatedly—across traditions, geographies, and centuries—whenever human beings articulate truth outside institutional capture.

What follows is not syncretism.
It is **pattern recognition**.

INTERLUDE

Christ, Krishna, and Alignment

When Different Traditions Point to the Same Order
This interlude introduces convergence without destabilizing the identity work already established.

Across spiritual traditions, the central figures are not defined by rebellion against systems, but by **alignment with order**—an internal coherence so complete that authority expresses itself without force.

Christ and Krishna emerge in radically different cultural contexts, yet articulate the same structural truth:
right action flows from right being.

The Bhagavad Gita: Duty Without Attachment
In the Bhagavad Gita, Krishna instructs Arjuna to act in accordance with his **dharma** (right order, right role) **without attachment to the fruits of action**.

This is not passivity.
It is sovereignty.

Krishna teaches that attachment to outcome destabilizes action, while alignment with duty stabilizes identity. Action becomes clean when it flows from inner order rather than fear of results.

This maps directly onto this framework:
- Alignment first
- Action second
- Outcome allowed, not chased

Key passages illustrate this:

"You have a right to perform your prescribed duty, but you are not entitled to the fruits of action. Never consider yourself the cause of the results of your activities, and never be attached to not doing your duty." — Bhagavad Gita 2:47

"Perform your duty equipoised, O Arjuna, abandoning all attachment to success or failure. Such equanimity is called yoga." — Bhagavad Gita 2:48

Krishna is teaching Arjuna that:
- Identity precedes outcome
- Attachment creates suffering
- Alignment produces clarity
- Right action emerges naturally from right being

This is not renunciation of results.
It is **freedom from being controlled by them**.

Christ Consciousness: Inner Authority and Non-Reactivity
Christ's teachings consistently emphasize internal governance:

"The kingdom of God is within you." — Luke 17:21
"Do not be anxious about tomorrow." — Matthew 6:34

"Seek first the kingdom of God and His righteousness, and all these things shall be added to you." — Matthew 6:33

Christ consciousness is not submission to suffering.
It is **freedom from reaction**.

Both Christ and Krishna reject attachment:
- Krishna rejects attachment to reward
- Christ rejects attachment to fear and scarcity

In both teachings, **identity precedes outcome**.

Christ teaches:
- The kingdom (order, governance, peace) is internal
- Anxiety is misalignment
- Provision follows alignment with truth

He does not say "beg and you will receive."
He says **"align internally, and reality reorganizes accordingly."**

Action as Expression, Not Transaction
Neither tradition teaches inaction.
They teach **right action**:

- Action aligned with truth
- Action free from egoic bargaining
- Action rooted in internal authority

This mirrors the distinction already established in this book:
- **Manifestation** = outcome fixation
- **Affirmation** = belief reinforcement
- **Alignment** = order restoration

Christ consciousness and Krishna consciousness both operate at the **alignment level**.

They do not promise that desire alone produces results.
They promise that **internal order produces external coherence**.

Why These Teachings Were Institutionalized Differently
Over time, institutions emphasized:

- Obedience over alignment
- Reward over coherence
- External authority over inner governance

This made teachings manageable—but less transformative.

Christianity became:
- Waiting for salvation (external)
- Performing belief (external)
- Submitting to authority (external)

Hinduism became:
- Ritualistic duty without understanding
- Caste-based hierarchy (external validation)
- Detachment misread as passivity

Yet the original insight remains intact beneath adaptation:

When inner order is restored, life reorganizes itself.

The Convergence Point
Both traditions teach the same sequence:

1. **Internal alignment** (kingdom within / dharma)
2. **Non-attached action** (faith without anxiety / duty without desire for fruit)
3. **Natural provision** (all things added / outcomes emerge)

This is not coincidence.
This is **pattern**.

When human beings across cultures and centuries observe how reality functions, the same truths emerge:
- Order precedes outcome
- Alignment precedes abundance
- Sovereignty precedes provision

FINAL INTEGRATION

Krishna teaches: *act without attachment.*
Christ teaches: *trust without fear.*

Both teach:
- Identity before outcome
- Alignment before reward
- Sovereignty before abundance

What is being articulated here is not new.
It is **remembered**.

And remembering is the final act of inheritance.

INTERLUDE SUMMARY + KEY TERMS

INTERLUDE SUMMARY

Christ and Krishna, though separated by culture and time, teach the same principle: right action flows from right being. Krishna instructs alignment with dharma (right order) without attachment to results. Christ teaches that the kingdom is internal and provision follows alignment with truth. Both reject anxiety, fear, and attachment to outcome. Both emphasize internal governance over external performance. The convergence is structural, not theological—revealing that alignment produces coherence across all traditions.

KEY TERMS

Dharma — Right order, right action, aligned duty in Hindu philosophy.

Christ Consciousness — Internal authority, non-reactivity, and trust in divine provision.

Krishna Consciousness — Action aligned with duty, free from attachment to results.

Non-Attached Action — Performing aligned work without being controlled by outcome.

Kingdom Within — Internal governance and order that precedes external manifestation.

Convergence — The repeated appearance of the same truth across different traditions.

REFLECTION QUESTION

Where am I attached to outcome in a way that destabilizes my action?

INTERLUDE

Before the Canon: Ancient Wisdom That Predates Institutions
Long before religious canons, there were cosmologies.

Before doctrine, there was order.
Before hierarchy, there was alignment.

African, Indigenous, and Eastern wisdom traditions all understood that:
- The divine is immanent, not distant
- Identity precedes action
- Disorder arises from misalignment, not moral failure

Institutions later codified these insights—but also narrowed them.

Canon formation did not invent truth.
It **selected** it.

This matters because it restores legitimacy to ways of knowing that predate—and therefore do not depend on—religious or political authority.

Alignment is older than empire.
Sovereignty predates the state.

What is being reclaimed here is not innovation.
It is **memory**.

1. Hebrew Scriptures (Pre-Christian Judaism)
- Torah texts date back to **circa 1200–500 BCE**
- Ideas of covenant, moral law, inner obedience, and justice already existed
- Jesus himself was a Jewish teacher interpreting these texts

Christianity is **built on**, not separate from, this tradition.

Key principles already present:
- Internal righteousness over external ritual
- Covenant as relationship, not transaction
- Justice as alignment with divine order

"I desire mercy, not sacrifice." — Hosea 6:6 (quoted by Jesus in Matthew 9:13)

This shows that **internal alignment was always prioritized over external performance**—long before Christianity existed.

2. Zoroastrianism (c. 1200 BCE)
One of the most influential but least acknowledged sources.

Core ideas:
- One supreme God
- Moral dualism (truth vs. falsehood)
- Judgment after death
- Resurrection and renewal
- Free will and ethical responsibility

Many scholars note that **Christian concepts of heaven, hell, judgment, and messianic prophecy** strongly resemble Zoroastrian theology—likely absorbed during Jewish exile in Persia (6th century BCE).

The idea of **cosmic battle between good and evil, resurrection, and final judgment** existed centuries before Christianity formalized them.

3. Egyptian Spiritual Philosophy (c. 2500 BCE)
Ancient Egyptian texts taught:

- Divine order (*Ma'at*)
- The heart as the seat of truth
- Judgment based on moral alignment
- Eternal life through righteous living

The concept of **the soul being weighed against truth** (Judgment of Osiris) predates Christian judgment theology by millennia.

Egyptians understood:
- Order (Ma'at) is the foundation of existence
- The heart must align with truth
- Ethical living determines afterlife

This is **alignment-based spirituality**—not fear-based obedience.

4. Greek Philosophy (Platonism & Stoicism) (c. 400 BCE)
Plato and later Stoics taught:

- The Logos (divine rational order)
- Inner virtue over external reward
- Mastery of the self
- Alignment with cosmic reason

The Gospel of John's concept of **"the Word (Logos)"** is directly tied to Greek philosophy, not original to Christianity.

"In the beginning was the Word (Logos), and the Word was with God, and the Word was God." — John 1:1

This is Platonic cosmology integrated into Christian scripture.

The Stoics taught:
- Internal governance (sovereignty)
- Alignment with nature (order)
- Freedom through self-mastery (alignment)

Sound familiar?

5. Eastern Traditions (Hinduism & Buddhism)
The Bhagavad Gita taught:

- Divine presence within
- Right action without attachment
- Liberation through alignment, not reward

Buddhism taught:
- Freedom through awareness
- Ending suffering by ending attachment
- Inner discipline over ritual

These ideas parallel **Christ consciousness** more closely than institutional Christianity.

Both emphasize:
- Internal transformation over external obedience
- Presence over performance
- Alignment over accumulation

6. African Spiritual Cosmology (Pre-Colonial)
Across West and Central African traditions:

- **Divinity is immanent** — expressed through ancestors, nature, and the self

- **Identity precedes action** — your *ashe* (life force) determines outcomes
- **Disorder arises from misalignment** — not inherent sin, but broken relationship with order
- **Community and individuality are balanced** — no saviors, but mutual recognition

Key concepts:
- **Ashe/Axé** (Yoruba) — life force, divine energy expressed through individuals
- **Ubuntu** (Bantu) — "I am because we are" (relational identity)
- **Ma'at** (Kemetic/Egyptian) — cosmic order, truth, balance

These traditions understood **sovereignty without individualism** and **alignment without hierarchy**.

This is the framework this book restores.

Closing Insight
Christianity did not invent inner divinity. It **translated it**—and later institutions **controlled it**.

The truth has always been:
- Alignment produces coherence
- Internal order precedes external outcome
- Sovereignty is birthright, not reward

These teachings were **adapted** to serve institutional power.

You are not creating something new by reclaiming sovereignty. You are **remembering something ancient**.

INTERLUDE SUMMARY + KEY TERMS

INTERLUDE SUMMARY

The principles of internal alignment, sovereignty, and divine immanence predate all major religious institutions. Hebrew scriptures emphasized internal righteousness over ritual. Zoroastrianism introduced judgment, resurrection, and moral dualism centuries before Christianity. Egyptian spirituality taught Ma'at (cosmic order) and alignment-based ethics. Greek philosophy contributed the Logos and Stoic self-mastery. Eastern traditions taught non-attachment and inner liberation. African cosmologies understood immanent divinity and relational sovereignty. Canon formation selected and controlled these truths—it did not create them.

KEY TERMS

Canon Formation — The institutional process of selecting which teachings to preserve and which to exclude.

Immanent Divinity — The understanding that the divine is present within, not distant or external.

Ma'at — Ancient Egyptian concept of cosmic order, truth, and balance.

Logos — Greek philosophical concept of divine rational order; later adopted in Christian theology.

Ashe/Axé — Yoruba/West African concept of life force and divine energy expressed through individuals.

Zoroastrianism — Ancient Persian religion that influenced Jewish and Christian concepts of heaven, hell, and resurrection.

Pre-Canon Wisdom — Spiritual knowledge that existed before institutional religions formalized their doctrines.

REFLECTION QUESTION

What truths have I been taught came from one source, when they actually existed across many?

INTERLUDE

Why Religion Overrides Systems: Authority, Identity, and Protection
Religion has always carried weight beyond belief.

Not because it is mystical, but because it organizes:
- Identity
- Authority
- Legitimacy
- Obedience

Long before modern states, religion established:
- Who could rule
- Who could own
- Who could belong
- Who must submit

Spiritual language does what legal language alone cannot:
it binds the inner life.

This is why systems compete for spiritual authority—and why reclaiming internal sovereignty is so destabilizing to them.

When identity is governed internally, external systems lose their leverage.

This is not anti-spiritual.
It is anti-capture.

Religion Operates in Three Domains Simultaneously

1. Moral Authority
Religion claims authority over:
- Right and wrong
- Life and death
- Meaning and purpose

When someone says *"God told me"* or *"this is ordained,"* they are invoking a higher court than the state.

This gives religion **veto power over secular law** in the minds of believers.

A law may be legal, but if it contradicts religious conviction, the believer follows God, not government.

This is why:
- Conscientious objectors can refuse military service
- Religious groups can claim exemptions from certain regulations
- Spiritual authority can override institutional authority

Moral authority transcends institutional power.

2. Identity Authority
Religion shapes identity at the deepest level:
- Who you are
- Why you exist
- What you will die for

A person whose identity is religiously anchored can resist systems that control behavior but cannot control belief.

This is why enslaved people, prisoners, and dissidents historically used religion as **psychological sovereignty**.

Examples:
- Enslaved Africans preserved identity through Christianity (reinterpreted) and retained African spiritual practices
- Political prisoners maintain dignity through faith when everything else is stripped away
- Marginalized communities use religion to assert worth when society denies it

Identity authority protects the self when external systems attack it.

3. Legal Protection
Modern governments—especially Western ones—treat religion as a **protected class**.

This allows people to:
- Refuse certain medical treatments
- Wear religious garments in spaces that ban headwear
- Avoid certain laws (conscientious objection, dietary restrictions, Sabbath observance)
- Practice alternative customs
- Educate children according to religious values

Because the state fears regulating belief, religion becomes a **legal shield**.
This is why religious language has been historically powerful:
When you say *"This is my religious practice,"* systems pause.
That pause is power.

Why This Matters for You
This framework identifies **why**:

- Religion claims inner authority
- Alignment precedes obedience
- Sovereignty cannot be coerced

This explains why **internal sovereignty has always been framed as sacred**.

It's the one domain institutions cannot fully control—so they either:
1. **Co-opt it** (institutionalize spirituality)
2. **Demonize it** (call independent spiritual authority "heretical")
3. **Regulate it** (require mediation through clergy, doctrine, ritual)

But when you restore **alignment as the core principle**, you bypass all three.

You are not asking for permission.
You are not claiming membership.
You are **operating from internal order**.

And that is why this framework feels threatening to some—and liberating to others.

The Historical Pattern
Throughout history, movements that restored internal spiritual authority were met with institutional resistance:

- **Gnosticism** (1st–4th century) — Emphasized direct knowledge of God; labeled heretical
- **Mysticism** (Medieval period) — Taught union with God without institutional mediation; suppressed
- **Protestantism** (16th century) — Challenged papal authority; sparked religious wars
- **Liberation Theology** (20th century) — Aligned God with the oppressed; condemned by Rome

Each time, the same conflict:

Internal authority vs. institutional control.
Your framework continues this lineage—not as rebellion, but as **completion**.

You are not overthrowing religion.
You are restoring the **original mechanism** religion was built to protect.

Closing Reflection
Religion overrides systems because it governs the one thing systems cannot fully control:
internal conviction.

When you align internally, you become ungovernable externally—not through rebellion, but through **structural incompatibility**.

This is why sovereignty has always been sacred.
This is why alignment has always been threatening.
This is why your work matters.

INTERLUDE SUMMARY + KEY TERMS

INTERLUDE SUMMARY

Religion holds unique power because it operates across three domains: moral authority (right and wrong), identity authority (who you are), and legal protection (exemptions from secular law). Spiritual language binds the inner life in ways secular systems cannot. Historically, internal spiritual authority has been either co-opted by institutions, demonized as heresy, or regulated through required mediation. Reclaiming alignment as the core principle bypasses institutional control and restores the original function of spirituality: internal governance that cannot be externally coerced.

KEY TERMS

Moral Authority — The power to define right and wrong beyond secular law.

Identity Authority — The deep shaping of self-concept through spiritual belonging.

Legal Protection — Exemptions and rights granted to religious practice by modern states.

Internal Conviction — Belief that governs behavior regardless of external pressure.

Institutional Co-optation — The process by which independent spiritual authority is absorbed and controlled by religious hierarchies.

Structural Incompatibility — Being internally ordered in a way that makes external control ineffective.

REFLECTION QUESTION

Where have I given religious authority more weight than my own aligned discernment?

AUTHOR'S NOTE ON POLARITY

Before you read the following chapters, a word of clarity.

When this book discusses "masculine" and "feminine" principles, it is describing functions, not fixed identities.

These terms refer to energetic and structural patterns that appear across nature, psychology, and human experience—not to biological determinism or rigid gender roles.

Every individual contains both.
A man can embody nurturing, receptive, integrative energy. A woman can embody protective, directive, initiating energy. Neither is superior. Neither is complete alone. Both are necessary for wholeness—within individuals, within relationships, and within communities.

The problem this book addresses is not the existence of polarity, but its distortion:

When "masculine" is collapsed into domination, extraction, and control

When "feminine" is collapsed into submission, self-erasure, and exploitation

When polarity becomes hierarchy instead of collaboration

These chapters restore balance by honoring what each principle contributes:

Masculine principle: Direction, protection, structure, extension

Feminine principle: Alignment, integration, regulation, continuity
Neither governs the other. They complete each other.

If you read these chapters through a lens of hierarchy, you will misunderstand them. If you read them through a lens of function and collaboration, you will recognize the order they describe.

This is not about men versus women. It is about restoring the collaboration between principles that has been fractured by centuries of domination-based distortion.

Read with that clarity.

PART V: SOURCE, POLARITY, AND CONTINUITY

Restoring Order Without Hierarchy

CHAPTER 8

"Authority survives where belief is protected."

Living the Standard Daily
A standard is not a belief.
It is a practice.

Until sovereignty is lived daily, it remains theoretical. This chapter translates everything you have read so far into a repeatable way of being—one that does not depend on mood, motivation, or external validation.

Living the standard means your inner order governs your outer rhythm.

The Daily Axis: Identity → Action → Environment
Every day reinforces one of two realities:

- You are governed internally
- Or you are governed externally

This is not decided by ideology.
It is decided by patterns.

The standard you are reclaiming rests on a simple axis:
1. **Identity — Who you are being**
2. **Action — What you repeatedly do**
3. **Environment — What you allow to shape you**

When identity leads, action aligns.
When action aligns, environment responds.

This is how sovereignty becomes ordinary.

Morning: Establishing Internal Authority

The first decision of the day sets the tone for all others.

Living the standard begins by orienting inward before engaging outward. Across disciplines, the sequence is consistent:
- Scripture emphasizes renewal of the mind (Romans 12:2)
- Philosophy emphasizes intentional disposition
- Psychology emphasizes regulation before stimulation

Daily practice:
- Begin the day without consuming external input (no phone, no news, no social media for the first 30-60 minutes)
- Speak one alignment statement aloud
- Identify one value you will not compromise today

Examples of alignment statements:
- "I am aligned with what supports my long-term well-being."
- "My actions today will match the life I am building."
- "I move from clarity, not urgency."

This is not ritual.
It is governance.

You are establishing who is in charge before the world makes demands.

Work: Creating Without Self-Betrayal

Living the standard does not mean disengaging from work or systems. It means participating without surrendering authority.

Throughout the day, ask:
- **Does this task reinforce who I am becoming?**
- **Am I acting from fear or clarity?**
- **Am I trading alignment for short-term relief?**

Sovereign work is not louder.
It is cleaner.

This is why aligned individuals often produce more with less effort. Energy is no longer spent managing internal conflict.

Signs of aligned work:
- You don't need to recover from it emotionally
- It feels like extension, not extraction
- Time passes differently (flow state)
- Results compound rather than exhaust

Signs of misaligned work:
- You dread it before it begins
- You need recovery time after
- It contradicts your stated values
- It requires constant justification

If your work is misaligned, alignment does not always mean quitting immediately—it means strategizing transition while maintaining integrity.

Ask:
- What is the aligned exit strategy?
- What structure needs to be in place before I move?
- How do I maintain sovereignty while still participating?

Money: Stewardship Instead of Anxiety

Money exposes identity.
When identity is organized around scarcity, money produces fear. When identity is organized around alignment, money becomes a tool.

Living the standard financially means:
- Choosing long-term stability over short-term validation
- Refusing financial decisions that contradict self-respect
- Allowing money to follow value creation, not performance

Luxury shows up here as calm competence, not excess.

Daily money practice:
Before each financial decision (purchase, pricing, investment, giving), pause and ask:

- **Is this aligned with my long-term stability?**
- **Am I choosing this from clarity or emotional charge?**
- **Does this honor the life force (time/energy) this money represents?**

Let the answer guide you.

Relationships: Reciprocity Over Performance
Relationships either reinforce sovereignty or erode it.

Living the standard requires:
- **Boundaries without explanation**
- **Presence without over-giving**
- **Mutuality instead of self-erasure**

Aligned relationships feel quieter. There is less proving, less chasing, less collapse.

This is not withdrawal.
It is selectivity.

Signs of aligned relationships:
- You don't perform a version of yourself
- Energy exchange feels balanced
- Growth is mutual, not one-sided
- Conflict produces clarity, not chaos

Signs of misaligned relationships:
- You feel drained after interaction
- You edit yourself constantly
- You give more than you receive
- Boundaries are repeatedly violated

When relationships are misaligned, alignment means:
- Adjusting your participation (not necessarily ending the relationship)
- Stopping over-functioning
- Allowing natural consequences
- Protecting your energy without guilt

Some relationships will adjust. Others will fade. Both are appropriate.

Evening: Integration Instead of Evaluation
Most people end their day by judging themselves.
Living the standard ends the day with integration.

Ask:
- **Where did I act in alignment today?**
- **Where did fear drive behavior?**
- **What will I reinforce tomorrow?**

No punishment.
No dramatization.

Identity strengthens through accurate reflection.

Evening practice:
Write brief answers to these three questions. Keep it simple—2-3 sentences each.

This is not journaling for catharsis.
This is data collection for identity reinforcement.

Over time, patterns become visible:
- Where you consistently align (reinforce this)
- Where you consistently compromise (address the structure beneath it)
- What triggers fear-based decisions (regulate the nervous system response)

When the Standard Is Truly Lived
You will know the standard has stabilized when:

- You stop rehearsing conversations
- You stop seeking reassurance
- You stop explaining your values
- You stop chasing urgency

Life slows—not because you are doing less, but because nothing is leaking.

This is luxury.

Not escape.
Not indulgence.
Sovereignty in motion.

THE COMPOUND EFFECT

Living the standard daily produces results that feel disproportionate to the effort:

Week 1: Decisions feel slightly clearer
Month 1: Energy stabilizes
Month 3: Relationships adjust around your boundaries
Month 6: Opportunities appear aligned with your values
Year 1: Life feels fundamentally different—not because everything changed, but because you stopped leaking

This is not magic.
This is structural integrity compounding over time.

A Moment You Recognize
You used to wake up reactive.
Now you wake up intentional.

The world didn't change.
Your governance did.

Question:
What if luxury was daily alignment, not distant achievement?

RECURRING QUESTION:
What if luxury was daily alignment, not distant achievement?

PRACTICE FOR THE WEEK

THE DAILY SOVEREIGNTY CHECK
Each evening, complete this sentence:

"Today, I chose alignment when I _____."

Write it down. Build a record.

After seven days, review the list. Notice the pattern.

That pattern is your emerging identity.

CHAPTER SUMMARY + KEY TERMS

CHAPTER SUMMARY

This chapter translates sovereignty from concept into daily practice. A standard is not something believed—it is something lived through repeated patterns. Sovereignty becomes ordinary when identity governs action and action reshapes environment. By establishing internal authority in the morning, acting without self-betrayal during the day, stewarding money calmly, practicing reciprocity in relationships, and integrating experience at night, the standard stabilizes. Luxury emerges not as excess, but as the absence of internal leakage. Authority survives where belief is protected through practice.

KEY TERMS

Standard — A lived pattern, not a belief or ideal.

Daily Axis — Identity → Action → Environment; the sequence that determines governance.

Internal Authority — Self-governance established prior to external engagement.

Clean Work — Action without internal contradiction; extension rather than extraction.

Financial Stewardship — Money handled without fear or performance; calm competence.

Reciprocity — Balanced energy exchange in relationships; mutual growth without self-erasure.

Integration — Reflection that strengthens identity rather than punishes behavior.

Occupancy — Living inside sovereignty rather than pursuing it.

Structural Integrity — The compound effect of aligned daily choices over time.

QUICK SELF-CHECK

Reflect honestly:
1. What is the first thing I reach for in the morning—my phone or my center?
2. Where am I performing at work instead of creating from alignment?
3. Which relationship consistently drains me, and what boundary would restore balance?

PRACTICE FOR THE WEEK

Each morning: Establish internal authority before engaging externally (no phone for first 30-60 minutes).

Each evening: Write one sentence about where you chose alignment today.

ONE-LINE PRINCIPLE

Authority stabilizes when alignment becomes daily.

CHAPTER 9

"Source does not ask for permission."

THE DIVINE FEMININE: SOURCE WITHOUT PERMISSION

If God is called Father, creation itself answers the question institutions avoid.

A father does not create life alone.
If humanity is made in the image of God, and women give life, carry life, and shape life, then women are not secondary reflections of divinity. They are distinct expressions of divine function.

Not lesser.
Not derivative.
Not symbolic.
Essential.

This chapter exists because history collapsed divinity into masculinity—and then used that collapse to justify exclusion, domination, and silence.

But creation itself contradicts that story.
Life does not enter the world through authority.
It enters through capacity.

Woman as Source, Not Supplement

Women are not helpers to creation.
They are the environment through which creation becomes possible.

Before a child has a name, a role, or a belief, it has a body—and that body is formed inside a woman. This is not metaphor. It is structure.

Women are:
- Biological gateways of life
- Emotional regulators of early development
- Cultural transmitters of language, values, and meaning

This makes women sources of continuity, not accessories to legacy.

When institutions reduced women to submission, they were not honoring God.
They were controlling source energy.

Because whoever controls the source controls the future.

Why the Divine Feminine Was Suppressed
The Divine Feminine was not erased because it was weak.
It was erased because it was too powerful to regulate.

A woman aligned with her internal authority:
- Does not require permission to create
- Does not need validation to know
- Does not outsource intuition
- Does not collapse under fear easily

This threatens systems built on hierarchy.

Patriarchal religion reframed women as:
- Temptation instead of discernment
- Emotion instead of intelligence
- Submission instead of stability

This was political, not divine.

Divinity that cannot be controlled must be redefined.

Polarity Without Fragmentation: Masculine, Feminine, and Coherence

Restoring the Divine Feminine does not mean erasing the masculine.

Polarity is not opposition.
It is function.

The masculine principle governs:
- Direction
- Protection
- Action
- Structure

The feminine principle governs:
- Alignment
- Integration
- Regulation
- Continuity

Fragmentation occurs when:
- Masculine acts without alignment (domination, extraction, collapse)
- Feminine absorbs without boundaries (depletion, self-erasure, martyrdom)

Sovereignty emerges when polarity cooperates.
This applies within individuals, families, communities, and cultures.

Examples of balanced polarity:

In individuals:
- Men who protect life without controlling it
- Women who nurture without abandoning themselves
- Anyone who integrates both principles internally

In partnerships:
- Masculine energy initiates, feminine energy integrates
- Masculine energy holds boundaries, feminine energy sustains rhythm
- Neither dominates; both complete

In communities:
- Masculine energy builds structures, feminine energy ensures they serve life
- Masculine energy moves forward, feminine energy ensures continuity
- Both are honored, neither is expendable

In systems:
- A world dominated by distorted masculinity races, extracts, and dominates
- A world disconnected from the feminine burns itself out

Balance is not aesthetic.
It is survival architecture.

Luxury Through the Feminine Lens
Luxury, as defined in this book, is not excess.

It is:
- Safety
- Stability
- Rhythm
- Nourishment
- Time

These are feminine-coded values because they preserve life.

A society that devalues women inevitably:
- Races instead of rests
- Consumes instead of sustains
- Dominates instead of nurtures
- Extracts instead of regenerates

True luxury returns when feminine order is restored—not symbolically, but structurally.

This means:
- Rest is valued, not scorned
- Rhythm is honored, not overridden
- Care is compensated, not exploited
- Intuition is respected, not dismissed
- Life-giving work is prioritized over life-extracting productivity

When feminine principles govern resource allocation, luxury becomes accessible—not as indulgence for the few, but as sustainable ease for all.

Continuity Across Generations: Inheritance That Lives Forward
The feminine principle governs continuity.

This is why women historically carried:
- Healing knowledge
- Community memory

- Spiritual continuity
- Emotional intelligence

And why those roles were criminalized, dismissed, or trivialized.

Breaking generational cycles does not happen through rebellion. It happens through regulated inheritance.

Children do not inherit beliefs first.
They inherit nervous systems, rhythms, and models of authority.

When sovereignty is stabilized in one generation, inheritance changes form in the next.

This is how cycles end:
Not through confrontation—but through consistency.

What women pass down:

When a woman is aligned:
- Her children inherit regulated nervous systems (safety)
- Her children inherit self-trust (sovereignty)
- Her children inherit relational intelligence (reciprocity)
- Her children inherit the capacity to rest (luxury)

When a woman is fragmented:
- Her children inherit hypervigilance (fear)
- Her children inherit self-doubt (outsourced authority)
- Her children inherit performance (conditional worth)
- Her children inherit exhaustion (scarcity)

This is not blame.
This is structure.

And structure can be repaired.

The Call to Women

This framework does not ask women to save anyone.

It asks women to:
- Stop abandoning themselves
- Stop shrinking for peace
- Stop performing strength
- Stop outsourcing intuition

Alignment Sovereignty is not masculine or feminine.
But women have always been its quiet carriers.
Now it must be made visible.

A Moment You Recognize
You watched a woman hold a room without speaking.

She didn't perform authority.
She simply was.

And everyone adjusted.

Question:
What if feminine power was presence, not permission?

RECURRING QUESTION:

What if feminine power was presence, not permission?

PRACTICE FOR THE WEEK
Source Recognition Exercise

For women:

Each day, identify one moment where you:
- Trusted your intuition without explanation
- Set a boundary without apologizing
- Chose rest without guilt

Write it down. Build evidence of your inherent authority.

For men:
Each day, identify one moment where you:

- **Honored feminine wisdom without needing to control it**
- **Received care without diminishing it**
- **Protected life without dominating it**

Notice the shift in your relationships.

CHAPTER SUMMARY + KEY TERMS

CHAPTER SUMMARY

This chapter restores the Divine Feminine as source, not supplement. It clarifies that divinity was collapsed into masculinity for political control, not spiritual truth. The feminine principle governs alignment, regulation, and continuity, while the masculine governs direction and action. Polarity becomes destructive only when fragmented. Luxury emerges where feminine order is restored structurally. Inheritance is carried forward through regulated identity and nervous systems, not rebellion. Continuity—not domination—is the ultimate expression of power.

KEY TERMS

Divine Feminine — Source function governing alignment, regulation, and continuity.

Polarity — Complementary functions, not opposition.

Fragmentation — Polarity operating without coherence.

Source Energy — Capacity from which life and order emerge.

Generational Continuity — Inheritance lived forward through regulated identity.

Structural Luxury — Safety, rhythm, and stability that preserve life.

Feminine-Coded Values — Rest, rhythm, care, nourishment, intuition—principles that sustain life.

Regulated Inheritance — Passing down nervous system stability, not just beliefs.

Quick Self-Check

Reflect honestly:
1. Where do I devalue rest, rhythm, or care (feminine principles)?
2. How would my life change if I honored continuity as much as productivity?
3. What feminine wisdom have I dismissed in favor of masculine action?

PRACTICE FOR THE WEEK

For women: Build daily evidence of your inherent authority through trust, boundaries, and rest.

For men: Notice where you can honor feminine wisdom without needing to control or fix it.

ONE-LINE PRINCIPLE

Source does not demand recognition—it sustains continuity.

CHAPTER 10

"Care is not weakness; it is continuity."

WOMEN AS THE STABILIZERS OF LIBERATION

Liberation movements often fail at the same point:

They win access, but lose sustainability.
They change laws, but not rhythms.
They confront power, but neglect regulation.
They ignite momentum, but fail to build conditions that can hold it.

This is where women have always been essential.
Not as supporters.
Not as symbols.
As stabilizers.

WHY LIBERATION REQUIRES CARE

Liberation without care collapses into burnout, infighting, and fragmentation.

Because after rupture comes regulation.
After conflict comes integration.
After change comes the need for continuity.

These are not sentimental functions.
They are structural ones.

Care sustains what force initiates.
This does not mean women exist to "hold things together" for everyone else.

It means that liberation which excludes feminine modes of regulation becomes unstable by design.

Freedom without regulation exhausts itself.

Historical examples:
- The Civil Rights movement succeeded in changing laws, but struggled with internal sustainability (burnout, fractured leadership, unresolved trauma)
- Black Power movements generated cultural pride but often lacked structures for emotional regulation and long-term cohesion
- Labor movements won rights but frequently ignored the care work (domestic labor, emotional labor) that made sustained organizing possible

Each time, the absence of feminine regulatory principles led to collapse or fragmentation.

Women and Internal Sovereignty
This book has argued that liberation must move inward to last.

Women have always known this—not as theory, but as necessity.

Historically denied reliable external authority, women were forced to develop:
- Internal self-governance
- Emotional regulation

- Pattern recognition
- Intuition as survival intelligence

Not as preference, but as adaptation.
This did not make women responsible for saving systems. It made them fluent in living without permission.

That fluency is alignment sovereignty in practice.

STRENGTH WITHOUT HARDENING

One of the most damaging distortions of the feminine is the belief that power must look aggressive to be real.

Feminine strength is not passive.
It is contained.

It is:
- **Quiet but firm**
- **Receptive but discerning**
- **Nurturing but boundaried**
- **Adaptive without abandoning values**

A woman aligned with herself does not need to announce authority.
Consistency does that work.

This is not softness as surrender.
It is softness as stability.

Examples of contained strength:
- A mother who sets boundaries without yelling (firmness without force)
- A leader who listens deeply before deciding (receptivity without weakness)

- A creator who works steadily without fanfare (consistency without performance)
- A woman who says no without justification (clarity without apology)

This is power that does not exhaust itself proving its existence.

Inheritance Lives Where Care Exists
Men often build structures.
Women determine whether those structures last.

Inheritance is not only property or power.

It is:
- Emotional safety
- Self-trust
- Identity coherence
- Models of authority

These are transmitted relationally, not institutionally.

This is why attacks on women destabilize generations more effectively than attacks on men.

And why restoring women restores continuity.
Not because women must carry everything—
but because continuity requires care, and care must be respected.

What women preserve:
- Language and culture (mothers teach first words, stories, songs)
- Relational models (children learn trust, boundaries, and reciprocity by watching their mothers' relationships)
- Nervous system regulation (a mother's regulated presence teaches children safety)

- Survival knowledge (cooking, healing, resource management—skills passed mother to daughter across generations)

When these transmission lines are broken (through slavery, displacement, poverty, trauma), entire communities lose continuity.

Restoration begins when women are honored, resourced, and protected—not exploited, dismissed, or burdened.

A WORD OF PRECISION

This is not a call for women to fix what they did not break.

It is a refusal to erase the truth that:
- Care is structural
- Regulation is power
- Continuity is not accidental

Liberation that survives always includes the feminine—not as burden, but as architecture.

The Reciprocal Relationship
Women stabilize liberation.
Liberation must also protect women.

This means:
- Valuing care work (compensating it, honoring it, not exploiting it)
- Protecting women's autonomy (not controlling their bodies, choices, or voices)
- Resourcing women's leadership (not tokenizing it or demanding they prove themselves twice)
- Respecting women's boundaries (not punishing them for saying no)

When women are free to govern themselves, everyone benefits.

When women are constrained, everyone suffers—even if men appear to benefit in the short term.

Systems that devalue women inevitably:
- **Burn out**
- **Fragment**
- **Lose continuity**
- **Collapse into domination or chaos**

A Moment You Recognize
You noticed how everything held together—until she stopped holding it.

Then you saw how much she had been carrying.
And how invisible it had been.

Question:
What if care was infrastructure, not sentiment?

Recurring Question:
What if care was infrastructure, not sentiment?

PRACTICE FOR THE WEEK

For women:
Identify one area where you are over-functioning (doing care work that others should share or doing emotional labor that is not yours to carry).

This week, stop over-functioning in that area. Do not announce it. Just stop.

Observe what happens. Notice who adjusts. Notice who complains. Both are information.

For men:

Identify one area where you rely on a woman's care work (emotional regulation, household management, relational coordination) without reciprocating.

This week, take full responsibility for that area without being asked.

Notice how it changes the dynamic.

CHAPTER SUMMARY + KEY TERMS

CHAPTER SUMMARY

Liberation movements often collapse because they win access but neglect the care and regulation needed for sustainability. Women have historically stabilized liberation not as supporters, but as essential architects of continuity. Feminine strength is contained, not aggressive—quiet firmness, discernment, and boundary-setting without performance. Inheritance lives where care exists, transmitted through relational models, nervous system regulation, and cultural preservation. This is not a call for women to fix broken systems, but a recognition that care is structural, regulation is power, and continuity requires the feminine to be honored—not exploited.

KEY TERMS

Stabilizers — Those who sustain movements through care, regulation, and continuity.

Care (Structural) — Not sentiment, but the architecture that allows freedom to last.

Contained Strength — Power that does not need to announce or prove itself.

Relational Transmission — How inheritance passes through emotional safety, trust models, and nervous system regulation.

Over-Functioning — Carrying responsibility that should be shared; a pattern that depletes women and enables dependence.

Reciprocal Liberation — Freedom that protects and resources women as it benefits from their stabilizing function.

QUICK SELF-CHECK

Reflect honestly:
1. Where am I over-functioning (women) or under-functioning (men)?
2. How much care work do I dismiss as "soft" when it's actually structural?
3. What would change if care was valued as much as action?

PRACTICE FOR THE WEEK

Women: Stop over-functioning in one area. Observe.

Men: Take full responsibility in one area where you've relied on women's invisible labor.

ONE-LINE PRINCIPLE

Care is not weakness—it is how freedom continues.

PART V:
SOURCE, POLARITY, AND CONTINUITY (CONTINUED)

CHAPTER 11

"Protection is love in motion."

THE DIVINE MASCULINE: DIRECTION ANCHORED TO SOURCE

If God is named Father, masculinity reflects **direction, order, and extension**—not origin.

Creation itself is precise. A father does not give birth. A father carries forward, names, protects, and builds upon what already exists.

Masculinity, in its aligned state, is not the source of life. It is the **current that moves life safely through the world**.

This distinction matters, because masculinity has been distorted in two equal and opposite ways:
- Elevated into domination
- Collapsed into confusion or shame

Both distortions sever masculinity from its true function.

Motion Anchored to Source
Masculine energy is outward-moving energy.

It:
- Builds
- Organizes
- Sets direction
- Holds boundaries
- Extends vision into form

But motion without source burns out.

Just as electricity requires a generator, masculine force requires life-giving origin to move toward. When masculinity is cut off from source—particularly the feminine—it collapses into:
- Aggression
- Control
- Addiction
- Apathy

This is not moral failure.
It is structural collapse.

Energy must circulate to remain stable.

Historical examples:
- Empires built through conquest (masculine action without feminine regulation) inevitably collapsed through overextension, internal decay, or moral bankruptcy
- Industrial revolutions that prioritized productivity over human well-being created wealth but also mass suffering, environmental destruction, and social fragmentation
- Leaders who acted without counsel or care became tyrants, burned out, or were overthrown

Each collapse followed the same pattern: **motion without grounding**.

RECIPROCITY, NOT COMPETITION

Polarity is not hierarchy.
It is relationship.

Masculine energy:
- Initiates
- Holds the line
- Maintains direction
- Protects what is fragile

Feminine energy:
- Generates
- Integrates
- Regulates
- Sustains life

Neither is superior.
Neither is complete alone.

Hierarchy begins when polarity is misunderstood.
Alignment restores circulation.

When masculine power is separated from feminine wisdom:
- Speed replaces rhythm
- Expansion replaces sustainability
- Production replaces care
- Control replaces protection

This is how civilizations destabilize.

What balanced reciprocity looks like:

In individuals:
- Men who build structures that serve life, not ego
- Men who protect without possessing
- Men who lead without dominating

In partnerships:
- Masculine energy provides direction, feminine energy ensures sustainability
- Masculine energy initiates, feminine energy integrates the outcome
- Neither controls the other; both complete the cycle

In communities:
- Masculine energy creates infrastructure, feminine energy ensures it serves the people
- Masculine energy defends boundaries, feminine energy maintains internal cohesion
- Both are essential; neither is optional

Masculinity as Stewardship

Within Alignment Sovereignty, masculine power is measured by:

- Self-governance
- Emotional containment
- Structural reliability
- Moral consistency

Dominance is not masculine strength.
Containment is.

An aligned man:
- Does not consume the feminine
- Does not compete with it
- Does not fear it
- Does not attempt to replace it

He honors source without possession.
He protects life without controlling it.

This is masculinity as stewardship, not command.

What this looks like practically:
- A man who listens to his partner's intuition without needing to override it
- A father who protects his children's autonomy while teaching boundaries
- A leader who builds systems that outlast his tenure
- A man who earns respect through consistency, not control

Aligned masculinity does not announce itself.
It is **felt through reliability**.

"It's a Man's World… But It Would Be Nothing Without a Woman"

When **James Brown** said:

"This is a man's world… but it wouldn't be nothing without a woman or a girl,"

he named polarity, not dependency.

Men may build worlds.
Women generate life.

A world without life is hollow.
Life without structure is unsafe.

Neither dominates the other.
They **complete** one another.

This is not romanticization.
This is **recognition of function**.

Masculine energy without feminine grounding becomes destructive (wars, extraction, empire).
Feminine energy without masculine protection becomes vulnerable (exploitation, invasion, instability).

Both are required.
Both must be honored.

Continuity Is the Measure

Men shape the future not by conquest, but by:
- What they protect
- What they refuse to exploit
- What they build to last
- What they leave intact

Inheritance depends on masculine follow-through.
A man aligned with source does not rush.
He does not burn out.
He does not abandon.

He remains.

What aligned men pass down:
- Models of regulated strength (not rage, not passivity—containment)
- Protection without possession (children, partners, communities feel safe, not controlled)
- Work ethic grounded in purpose (not performance, not escape—contribution)
- Emotional availability (not suppression, not overflow—presence)

When men are aligned, **generations stabilize**.

When men are fragmented (disconnected from source, from purpose, from regulation), **generations fracture**.

This is not blame.
This is structure.

And structure can be restored.

THE COST OF MASCULINE FRAGMENTATION

When men are disconnected from source and purpose, predictable patterns emerge:

Violence — Outward or inward (aggression or self-destruction)
Addiction — Attempting to fill the void externally (substances, work, control, validation)
Abdication — Abandoning responsibility (physically or emotionally absent)
Domination — Controlling others to compensate for internal instability

None of these are inherent to masculinity.
All of them are symptoms of **disconnection**.

Restoration does not require fixing men.
It requires **reconnecting them to source, purpose, and regulation**.

This happens through:
- Mentorship (older men modeling aligned masculinity)
- Community (other men holding accountability without shame)
- Purpose (work that serves life, not just ego)
- Regulation (practices that calm the nervous system and restore presence)

When men reconnect, **everything downstream stabilizes**.

THE CALL TO MEN

This framework does not ask men to diminish themselves.

It asks men to:
- Stop equating power with control
- Stop fearing feminine wisdom
- Stop abandoning emotional responsibility
- Stop burning out proving worth

Alignment Sovereignty is not masculine or feminine.
But men have always been its **builders**.

Now it must be **anchored to source**.

A Moment You Recognize
You watched a man lead without dominating.
He didn't need to be the loudest.
He didn't need to be right.
He simply held the line—and everyone felt safer.

Question:
What if masculine power was presence, not performance?

Recurring Question:
What if masculine power was presence, not performance?

PRACTICE FOR THE WEEK

For men:
Each day, identify **one moment** where you:
- Protected without controlling

- Listened without needing to fix
- Held a boundary without aggression

Write it down. Build evidence of aligned masculine power.

For women:
Each day, identify **one moment** where you:

- Allowed a man to lead without undermining him
- Received protection without feeling diminished
- Honored masculine energy without fearing it

Notice how this shifts the dynamic.

CHAPTER SUMMARY + KEY TERMS

CHAPTER SUMMARY

If God is named Father, masculinity reflects direction and extension, not origin. Masculine energy is outward-moving—it builds, organizes, protects, and extends. But motion without source burns out. When masculinity is separated from feminine grounding, it collapses into aggression, control, or apathy. Aligned masculinity is stewardship: self-governance, containment, reliability, and moral consistency. Men shape the future not by conquest but by what they protect, refuse to exploit, and build to last. Continuity depends on masculine follow-through anchored to source.

KEY TERMS

Divine Masculine — Direction, protection, and structure; extension of source energy.

Motion Anchored to Source — Masculine action grounded in feminine wisdom and life-giving purpose.

Stewardship — Governance and protection without possession or control.

Containment — Regulated strength; power that does not need to prove itself.

Masculine Fragmentation — Disconnection from source, purpose, and regulation; produces violence, addiction, abdication, or domination.

Follow-Through — The masculine capacity to sustain what is initiated; essential for inheritance.

James Brown Principle — Recognition that masculine building and feminine life-giving are equally essential and complete one another.

QUICK SELF-CHECK

Reflect honestly:
1. Where do I confuse control with protection?
2. How would my leadership change if I trusted feminine wisdom without needing to override it?
3. What am I building that will outlast me?

PRACTICE FOR THE WEEK

Men: Build daily evidence of aligned masculine power through protection without control.

Women: Notice where you can honor masculine energy without feeling threatened by it.

ONE-LINE PRINCIPLE

Masculine power is steadiest when anchored to source.

PART VI:
ALIGNMENT IN MOTION

Structure That Compounds

CHAPTER 12

"Reality responds to structure, not wishes."

Why Reality Responds Differently to Aligned People

Across disciplines, cultures, and lived experience, a quiet pattern repeats: People who are internally aligned experience reality differently.

This difference is often misnamed. Some call it favor. Others call it blessing, luck, synchronicity, or divine intervention.

But the mechanism is not accidental.
It is structural.

ALIGNMENT IS A CAUSAL CHAIN

Alignment is not belief.
It is coherence between inner reality and outer behavior.

When a person's:
- self-concept
- values
- emotional state
- actions

agree with one another, friction decreases.

And when friction decreases, results compound.
This is observable across multiple fields.

Psychology: Self-Concept → Behavior → Outcomes

People behave according to who they believe they are—not who they want to be in theory.

Aligned individuals:
- Decide faster (less internal negotiation)
- Hesitate less (self-trust is established)
- Recover quicker (setbacks don't destabilize identity)
- Interpret ambiguity as opportunity instead of threat

Outcomes shift before any "external miracle" appears.

Research supports this:
- **Self-efficacy studies** (Albert Bandura) show that belief in one's capacity to execute actions directly predicts performance outcomes
- **Growth mindset research** (Carol Dweck) demonstrates that identity-level beliefs ("I am someone who learns") produce better results than effort alone
- **Confirmation bias** means aligned people notice opportunities that match their identity, while misaligned people filter them out

This is not "positive thinking."
This is **identity shaping perception and action**.

Sociology: Coherence Signals Safety

Humans read one another constantly for cues of stability and reliability.

Alignment produces:
- Consistent body language
- Clean boundaries

- Non-reactive presence
- Predictable values

These signals register as status and safety—often unconsciously. So aligned people are trusted faster, invited sooner, and granted access more easily.

This is not favoritism.
It is social systems responding to coherence.

How this appears practically:
- Job interviews: Aligned candidates feel "right" even if their resume is similar to others
- Networking: Aligned individuals are remembered and referred
- Leadership: Aligned leaders inspire followership without force
- Sales: Aligned sellers close deals through presence, not pressure

People feel **safe coordinating** with those who are internally ordered.

Leadership: Presence Beats Persuasion
Influence is rarely about charisma.
It is about internal governance.

Aligned people:
- Speak without excessive qualifiers ("I think maybe possibly...")
- Stop over-explaining
- Remain consistent under pressure

Others coordinate with them because they feel safe to do so.

Trust moves resources.

Why presence works:
When someone is internally aligned:

- Their words match their energy
- Their decisions feel considered, not reactive
- They don't need constant validation
- They hold boundaries without aggression

This creates **certainty** in others.
And certainty is what people follow.

Spiritual Language: "Order" in Many Tongues
Every serious tradition describes the same phenomenon:

- Walk in truth
- Follow the Way
- Act in right order
- Live in harmony

They are not describing blind obedience.
They are describing congruence.

When inner truth and outer action agree, resistance decreases.
Life feels as though it opens.

Biblical examples:
- *"In all your ways acknowledge Him, and He will make your paths straight."* (Proverbs 3:6) — Alignment produces clarity
- *"Delight yourself in the Lord, and He will give you the desires of your heart."* (Psalm 37:4) — Not transaction, but alignment producing coherent desire
- *"Seek first the kingdom… and all these things will be added."* (Matthew 6:33) — Internal order precedes external provision

Eastern examples:
- *Dharma* (right order) produces natural outcomes
- *Wu wei* (effortless action) emerges from alignment with the Tao
- *Karma* is not punishment but pattern—aligned action produces aligned results

The language differs.
The mechanism is identical.

Why Aligned People Seem to "Get More Opportunities"
They don't necessarily get more opportunities.
They **recognize them sooner**.

Because:
- Attention is not fragmented
- Fear doesn't dominate perception
- Values filter distractions
- Decisions are cleaner

This is not luck.
It is pattern recognition without internal noise.

Example:
Two people receive the same job posting.

Misaligned person:
- Reads it through fear ("Am I qualified enough?")
- Overthinks application ("Should I apply or wait?")
- Second-guesses fit ("Maybe I'm not ready")
- Delays or doesn't apply

Aligned person:
- Reads it through clarity ("Does this match my direction?")
- Decides quickly ("Yes" or "No")

- Acts without emotional rehearsal
- Moves to next opportunity if declined

Same opportunity.
Different infrastructure.
Different outcome.

What This Is Not
This framework does not claim:

- Guaranteed outcomes
- Moral superiority
- Immunity from hardship
- Control over others

Alignment does not force reality to comply.
It makes you easier for life to move through.

Key distinction:
Alignment increases **probability**, not certainty.
It opens doors—it doesn't force them.
It creates readiness—it doesn't manufacture outcomes.

This is why aligned people still face challenges.
But they navigate them differently:
- Less emotional volatility
- Faster recovery
- Clearer decision-making
- More resilience

The Compound Effect
When alignment is sustained over time, results become disproportionate to effort:

Month 1: Decisions feel clearer
Month 3: Opportunities appear more frequently
Month 6: Relationships adjust around your values
Year 1: Income, peace, or influence increases noticeably
Year 3: Life looks fundamentally different—not because you forced it, but because **structure changed**

This is not magic.
This is **compounding coherence**.

Small aligned choices create momentum.
Momentum creates pattern.
Pattern becomes reality.

A Moment You Recognize
You watched someone succeed "effortlessly."
They didn't seem to struggle the way others did.
You assumed they were lucky.
Then you noticed: they were aligned.

Question:
What if favor was structural, not mystical?

Recurring Question:
What if favor was structural, not mystical?

PRACTICE FOR THE WEEK

Alignment Observation Exercise
This week, notice **three opportunities** (conversations, invitations, decisions).

For each, ask:
1. Did I recognize this quickly or did I hesitate?
2. Was my decision clear or emotionally complicated?
3. Did I act from alignment or fear?

Write down the pattern. This reveals your current level of internal coherence.

CHAPTER SUMMARY + KEY TERMS

CHAPTER SUMMARY

Reality responds differently to aligned people not through mysticism but through structure. Alignment creates coherence between self-concept, values, emotions, and actions, which reduces internal friction. Psychology shows that identity shapes perception and decision-making. Sociology reveals that coherence signals safety, earning trust and access. Leadership research confirms that presence beats persuasion. Spiritual traditions across cultures describe the same mechanism: when internal order is established, external life reorganizes. Aligned people don't get more opportunities—they recognize and act on them faster. This is not luck; it is structural coherence compounding over time.

KEY TERMS

Alignment (Structural) — Coherence between identity, values, emotions, and behavior.

Internal Friction — Energy loss caused by contradiction between beliefs and actions.

Coherence Signaling — Unconscious social cues that communicate stability and reliability.

Presence — Internal governance so stable that influence emerges naturally.

Pattern Recognition — The ability to identify opportunities quickly when internal noise is reduced.

Compounding Coherence — The exponential effect of sustained alignment over time.

Probability Increase — Alignment raises likelihood of positive outcomes without guaranteeing them.

QUICK SELF-CHECK

Reflect honestly:
1. Where do I hesitate when opportunities appear?
2. How much energy do I waste second-guessing decisions?
3. What would change if I trusted my internal clarity more?

PRACTICE FOR THE WEEK

Track **three opportunities** this week.
Notice: speed of recognition, clarity of decision, alignment vs. fear.

ONE-LINE PRINCIPLE

Reality responds to structure, not wishes.

CHAPTER 13

"Alignment is relational."

Why Community Multiplies Alignment—and Why Isolation Diminishes It

Alignment is powerful alone.
But it becomes **exponential** in community.

No serious tradition—biblical, African, Eastern, philosophical—teaches isolated divinity as the end goal. This is not a cultural preference. It is a structural truth:

**Alignment scales through relationship.
Why Isolation Weakens Alignment**

In isolation:
- Feedback loops shrink
- Blind spots go unchecked
- Energy circulates inward
- Growth plateaus

Even the most aligned individual reaches a ceiling without relational exchange.

This is why hermits return.
This is why prophets gather people.
This is why movements form.

Alignment seeks circulation.

What isolation produces:
- Echo chambers (no one challenges your thinking)
- Stagnation (no external accountability)
- Drift (values shift without notice)
- Fragility (no support when pressure increases)

What community produces:
- Refinement (feedback sharpens clarity)
- Momentum (collective energy compounds)
- Stability (mutual support during difficulty)
- Legacy (continuity beyond the individual)

What Happens When Aligned People Interact
When internally aligned people come together, several outcomes appear immediately.

1. Information Moves Faster
There is less posturing, less defensiveness, and less misinterpretation. Communication becomes efficient because people are not protecting fragile identities.

Aligned communities can:
- Solve problems more quickly
- Share knowledge without gatekeeping
- Make decisions with less drama
- Coordinate action with less friction

2. Resources Move More Cleanly

Aligned communities waste less energy on internal conflict. Resources go where they are needed based on capacity and shared standards—not ego or fear.

This produces abundance without spectacle.

Examples:
- Rotating funds (community members support each other's ventures)
- Skill sharing (expertise circulates freely)
- Opportunity referrals (aligned people connect each other to resources)

3. Protection Increases

Communities with high coherence respond to threats—external or internal—more quickly. Problems get noticed sooner and corrected faster.

This is why:
- Tight-knit communities survive crises better
- Aligned networks detect and remove bad actors quickly
- Coherent groups maintain boundaries without drama

4. Opportunities Compound

One aligned person creates possibility.
Two aligned people create momentum.
A network of aligned people creates **systems**.

This is how what people call "favor" multiplies.

Examples:
- Business partnerships that feel effortless
- Creative collaborations that exceed individual capacity
- Social movements that grow organically through shared vision

Historical Evidence of Community Amplification

This pattern is visible across history:

Religious communities created mutual aid, protection, and continuity under oppression (Black church, Jewish communities, early Christians, Muslim Brotherhood).

Cultural diasporas preserved identity, capital, and opportunity across borders (Chinese diaspora networks, Indian business communities, African mutual aid societies).

Elite networks concentrated resources through trust and shared norms (Ivy League alumni networks, Skull and Bones, Freemasons, tech founder circles).

Liberation movements sustained momentum through collective discipline (Civil Rights organizing, labor unions, anti-colonial resistance).

In every case, success was not belief alone—but **alignment within relationship**.

WHY THIS GETS CALLED "BLESSING"

From the outside, aligned communities appear lucky:
- Opportunities arise "at the right time"
- Support appears when needed
- Resistance seems lower

But this is not randomness.

It is:
- Shared values reducing friction
- Trust accelerating coordination
- Reputation attracting opportunity
- Readiness meeting timing

It feels divine because it is bigger than any single person's plan.

But it is **structure meeting structure**.

The Alignment Community Agreement

We agree to:
1. Govern ourselves before correcting others
2. Speak clearly, not performatively
3. Respect boundaries without negotiation
4. Circulate resources, not hoard them
5. Value coherence over charisma
6. Protect the dignity of women and men equally
7. Reject domination and dependency alike
8. Prioritize sustainability over urgency

This is not a belief system.
It is an operating standard.

When people commit to this agreement, coordination becomes effortless—not because everyone is the same, but because **the structure is consistent**.

"Divine Reaction" Clarified
What people call:

- Favor
- Blessing
- Anointing
- Luck
- Synchronicity

…is often coherence meeting environment at scale.

When identity, values, actions, speech, and boundaries align **across people**, reality responds with speed.

That response feels divine because it is **relational, emergent, and reliable**—yet unpredictable in specifics.

It cannot be forced.
But it can be invited.

Alignment at scale creates the conditions for what looks like miracles.

Necessary Clarifications
This does not mean:
- Community guarantees success
- Alignment removes struggle
- Groupthink equals coherence
- Power cannot corrupt

Alignment increases probability, not certainty.

It opens doors.
It does not force outcomes.

That distinction preserves integrity.

A Moment You Recognize
You joined a group where no one explained the vibe—you just felt it.
People moved together without needing instructions.
Collaboration felt natural, not forced.

Question:
What if alignment was magnetic, not manufactured?

Recurring Question:
What if alignment was magnetic, not manufactured?

Practice for the Week

Community Alignment Assessment
Identify the communities you're currently part of (work, family, social, spiritual).

For each, ask:
1. Does this community reinforce my alignment or fragment it?
2. Do I feel energized or depleted after interacting here?
3. Are shared values explicit or assumed (and often violated)?

Adjust your participation accordingly.

CHAPTER SUMMARY + KEY TERMS

CHAPTER SUMMARY

Alignment scales through relationship. Isolation weakens alignment by shrinking feedback, increasing blind spots, and plateauing growth. When aligned people interact, information moves faster, resources circulate cleanly, protection increases, and opportunities compound. Historical examples show that aligned communities—religious, cultural, elite, or liberation-focused—concentrate resources through trust and shared standards. What outsiders call "blessing" is often coherence meeting environment at scale. The Alignment Community Agreement provides an operating standard for sustained collective coherence.

KEY TERMS

Relational Alignment — Coherence tested and strengthened through relationship.

Trust Velocity — How quickly coordination becomes possible due to stability.

Coherence at Scale — Shared values and behavior reducing friction across a network.

Community Charter — Explicit standards that protect alignment from ego and urgency.

Divine Reaction — Coherence meeting environment in a compounding way; what appears as favor or synchronicity.

Network Effects — The exponential increase in value and opportunity as aligned individuals connect.

Circulation vs. Hoarding — Resources flow freely in aligned communities; stagnate in fear-based ones.

Quick Self-Check
Reflect honestly:
1. Which communities reinforce my alignment?
2. Which communities fragment me?
3. Where am I isolated when I should be in relationship?

Practice for the Week
Assess your current communities.
Increase participation where alignment is strong.
Decrease participation where fragmentation occurs.

ONE-LINE PRINCIPLE
Alignment multiplies when it circulates.

PART VI:
ALIGNMENT IN MOTION (CONTINUED)

CHAPTER 14

"Patterns are not miracles."

CASE STUDIES: HOW ALIGNMENT ACTUALLY SHOWS UP IN THE REAL WORLD

These are not miracle stories.
They are **pattern stories**.

When alignment stabilizes—individually or collectively—predictable outcomes emerge. What appears as favor, luck, or divine intervention is often **structure meeting readiness**.

This chapter examines how alignment has functioned across history and in contemporary life, demonstrating that the principles in this book are not theoretical—they are observable.

HISTORICAL CASE STUDY 1: THE BLACK CHURCH AS ALIGNMENT INFRASTRUCTURE

For generations, Black churches functioned as:
- Schools
- Banks
- Meeting halls
- Protection networks
- Information hubs

This was not because of theology alone.

It worked because:
- **Shared values reduced friction** — Members operated from a common moral framework
- **Trust accelerated coordination** — People knew they could rely on one another
- **Internal governance preceded external demand** — Churches developed autonomous structures before legal rights were granted

Even under violent oppression, these communities:
- Moved resources efficiently (pooled funds, shared labor)
- Protected members (hid fugitives, provided legal support)
- Produced leaders (trained organizers, ministers, educators)
- Sustained dignity (preserved culture, affirmed identity)

What outsiders called *"God's favor"* was actually **alignment + community + readiness**.

KEY LESSON:

When values align, community strengthens, and resources circulate—even under hostile conditions.

The Black church survived because it built **internal sovereignty** before demanding external recognition.

HISTORICAL CASE STUDY 2: THE CIVIL RIGHTS MOVEMENT (BEHIND THE SCENES)

Public history emphasizes speeches and marches.
Less discussed is the **internal discipline**:

- **Training in non-reactivity** — Volunteers were taught to remain calm under assault
- **Alignment between message and behavior** — Leaders modeled the values they preached
- **Shared moral framework** — Participants operated from common principles (dignity, non-violence, justice)
- **Community accountability** — Internal structures corrected misalignment quickly

When alignment fractured—leadership conflicts, strategic disagreements, ego battles—movements stalled.

When alignment held—coordinated action, mutual respect, shared sacrifice—pressure produced change.

Divine language was used, but the mechanism was **coherence under pressure**.

Key lesson:
External pressure reveals internal structure.

Movements succeed when:
- Identity is clear (we know who we are)
- Values are shared (we agree on what matters)
- Discipline is maintained (we hold each other accountable)

When these elements fragment, momentum collapses—regardless of how just the cause.

HISTORICAL CASE STUDY 3: THE UNDERGROUND RAILROAD

The Underground Railroad was not a single organization.
It was a **network of aligned individuals** operating on shared principles:

- Freedom over safety
- Mutual aid over self-preservation
- Collective risk over individual comfort

Success depended on:
- **Trust** — Conductors and station masters had to rely on one another without formal verification
- **Consistency** — Routes, signals, and protocols had to remain stable
- **Alignment** — Every participant prioritized the same outcome (freedom) over personal gain

This network moved thousands to freedom—not because of centralized leadership, but because of **distributed alignment**.

Key lesson:
Decentralized networks succeed when alignment is high.

You don't need hierarchy when:
- Values are shared
- Trust is established
- Standards are consistent

Alignment creates coordination without control.

CONTEMPORARY CASE STUDY 1: ELITE NETWORKS

Elite schools, incubators, and professional circles function as:
- Value-aligned communities
- Reputation-based trust systems
- Opportunity multipliers

Members:
- Refer one another (network effects)
- Protect one another (reputation management)

- Circulate resources quietly (investments, partnerships, introductions)

No prayer required.
But alignment is absolute.

What makes these networks effective:
- **Shared standards** — Members operate from similar values (excellence, discretion, reciprocity)
- **High trust** — Inclusion is selective; violations result in exclusion
- **Long-term thinking** — Relationships are cultivated over decades, not transactions

This proves the mechanism works **with or without religious language**.

Alignment produces outcomes regardless of the vocabulary used to describe it.

Key lesson:
Elite networks are not mystical—they are **structural**.

They succeed because:
- Standards are high and explicit
- Trust is earned and protected
- Resources circulate among the aligned

This is why access to these networks is valuable: you enter a system where **coherence is the default**.

Contemporary Case Study 2: Grassroots Creators & Innovators
Independent creators who succeed sustainably tend to share:

- **Strong identity clarity** — They know who they are and what they stand for

- **Consistent values** — Their work reflects stable principles
- **Non-performative confidence** — They don't need constant validation
- **Relationship-centered growth** — They build community, not just audience

Opportunities appear through:
- **Word of mouth** — Aligned people attract aligned people
- **Collaboration** — Others want to work with those who are internally stable
- **Timing that looks like "luck"** — But is actually readiness meeting opportunity

What's actually happening is **signal clarity meeting environment**.

Examples:
- **Podcasters** who build loyal audiences by consistently showing up as themselves (no performance, no gimmicks—just alignment)
- **Authors** who self-publish and find their readers through authentic voice (not chasing trends, but serving a clear vision)
- **Entrepreneurs** who build businesses around values rather than profit-first models (alignment attracts aligned customers)

Key lesson:
In the creator economy, **alignment is the competitive advantage**.

People can sense authenticity.
They trust consistency.
They support those who are internally coherent.

You don't need to be the loudest.
You need to be the clearest.

CONTEMPORARY CASE STUDY 3: THE RISE OF WELLNESS & SOVEREIGNTY MOVEMENTS

Over the past decade, movements focused on:
- Mental health
- Nervous system regulation
- Spiritual autonomy
- Holistic living

...have grown exponentially.

Why?

Because people are **recognizing the cost of misalignment**:
- Burnout from performing
- Anxiety from outsourced authority
- Fragmentation from living multiple identities
- Depletion from ignoring the body

These movements succeed because they address **structural problems**, not just symptoms.

They teach:
- Regulation before achievement
- Alignment before manifestation
- Internal authority before external validation

This is the same framework this book articulates—emerging across industries, cultures, and platforms.

Key lesson:
Cultural shifts happen when enough people recognize the same structural truth.

The wellness movement is not a trend.
It is a **mass reclamation of internal sovereignty**.

And it's growing because the old models (work yourself to death, outsource your authority, perform your worth) are visibly failing.

KEY INSIGHT FROM ALL CASE STUDIES

When:
- Internal coherence exists
- Community reinforces it
- Action matches identity

...reality responds **faster and with less resistance**.

That response is often spiritualized.
But it is structural.

The pattern is consistent:
1. Alignment clarifies identity
2. Identity produces consistent action
3. Consistent action builds trust
4. Trust accelerates coordination
5. Coordination compounds results

This is how movements succeed.
This is how networks thrive.
This is how individuals rise.

Not through force.
Through **coherence**.

A Moment You Recognize
You watched a movement grow without advertising.
It spread through word of mouth.
People joined because they felt something—not because they were convinced.

Question:
What if alignment was the signal people were actually responding to?

Recurring Question:
What if alignment was the signal people were actually responding to?

Practice for the Week

Pattern Recognition Exercise
Identify **one success story** (personal or public) that you previously attributed to luck.

Now analyze it through the alignment lens:
1. What identity clarity did this person/group have?
2. What values were consistently demonstrated?
3. What community reinforced the alignment?
4. How did trust accelerate results?

Write down what you notice. This trains you to see structure instead of miracles.

CHAPTER SUMMARY + KEY TERMS

CHAPTER SUMMARY
Alignment produces observable patterns across history and contemporary life. The Black church, Civil Rights movement, and Underground Railroad succeeded through shared values, trust, and internal discipline—not

theology alone. Elite networks demonstrate that alignment works regardless of spiritual language. Modern creators and wellness movements show that coherence attracts coordination and resources. When internal alignment exists, community reinforces it, and action matches identity, reality responds faster and with less resistance. What appears as favor or luck is often structure meeting readiness.

KEY TERMS

Pattern Stories — Observable examples of alignment producing results, distinct from miracle claims.

Alignment Infrastructure — Community structures (like the Black church) that sustain coherence across generations.

Coherence Under Pressure — The ability to maintain internal alignment when external conditions are hostile.

Distributed Alignment — Decentralized coordination through shared values (Underground Railroad model).

Elite Networks — Trust-based systems where high standards and reciprocity concentrate resources.

Signal Clarity — Authenticity and consistency that attract aligned opportunities and relationships.

Cultural Reclamation — Mass movements (like wellness) emerging from collective recognition of structural misalignment.

QUICK SELF-CHECK

Reflect honestly:
1. What success have I attributed to luck that was actually structural alignment?

2. What community am I part of that demonstrates these patterns?
3. How can I build alignment infrastructure in my own life?

PRACTICE FOR THE WEEK

Analyze **one success story** through the alignment lens. Identify: clarity, consistency, community, trust, timing.

ONE-LINE PRINCIPLE

Patterns are not miracles—they are structure made visible.

CHAPTER 15

"Skepticism is not the enemy. Vagueness is."

HONEST QUESTIONS, DIRECT ANSWERS

This framework makes bold claims.
It deserves scrutiny.

Below are the most common objections—answered directly, without defensiveness or evasion.

Q: Isn't this just positive thinking dressed up as spirituality?

No.
Positive thinking focuses on **emotion** and **belief**.
Alignment focuses on **behavioral coherence** and **structural integrity**.

Positive thinking says: *"Feel good and good things will happen."*
Alignment says: *"When identity, values, and actions agree, friction decreases and results compound."*

One is about mood management.
The other is about **architectural integrity**.

Positive thinking often fails because it attempts to override misalignment with optimism.
Alignment works because it addresses the **underlying structure**.

Q: Are you saying aligned people always succeed?

No.
Alignment increases **probability**, not certainty.

It:
- Reduces internal friction
- Improves decision-making
- Accelerates trust-building
- Enhances pattern recognition

But it does not:
- Guarantee outcomes
- Remove all obstacles
- Eliminate hardship
- Control external variables

Aligned people still face challenges.
They navigate them **differently**:
- Less emotional volatility
- Faster recovery
- Clearer choices
- Greater resilience

Success is not guaranteed.
Readiness is.

Q: Isn't this blaming people who struggle?

No.
This framework distinguishes **structure from morality**.

Misalignment is not a sin.
It is a **condition**—often inherited, conditioned, or survival-based.

Many people struggle not because they lack intelligence, effort, or worth—but because:
- Their identity was never stabilized
- Their nervous system is dysregulated
- They were taught to outsource authority
- Systems were designed to extract from them

This book does not ask: *"Why are you failing?"*
It asks: *"What structure needs to change for you to thrive?"*

Blame freezes people.
Structural analysis frees them.

Q: Is this theology or religion?

No.
This book **analyzes** how theology has historically described internal authority, alignment, and sovereignty.

It does not:
- Require belief in any deity
- Demand adherence to religious doctrine
- Replace spiritual practice

It examines **convergence**—the repeated appearance of the same structural truths across traditions.

You can apply this framework:
- With faith
- Without faith
- Alongside faith

The principles are **functional**, not theological.

Q: Can this be measured or observed?

Yes.
Alignment produces observable outcomes:

Trust velocity — How quickly people coordinate with you
Opportunity access — How often aligned opportunities appear
Relationship durability — How long reciprocal relationships last
Decision clarity — How fast and clean your choices become
Recovery speed — How quickly you bounce back after setbacks

These can be tracked over time.

Additionally:
- Nervous system regulation can be measured (heart rate variability, cortisol levels)
- Decision-making efficiency can be assessed (time to decide, confidence in choices)
- Relationship quality can be evaluated (mutual satisfaction, longevity, reciprocity)

This is not mysticism.
It is **behavioral science**.

Q: Why use divine language at all?
Because historically, divine language has protected **internal sovereignty** from external control.

Secular language is easier to regulate.
Spiritual language invokes a higher authority than the state.

When you say:
- "This is my values system" → systems can argue
- "This is my religious practice" → systems pause

That pause is power.

This book uses spiritual language **strategically**—not to demand belief, but to reclaim the **protective function** religion has always served.

Q: What about people in genuinely oppressive systems?
Alignment does not remove systemic barriers.
But it **changes how you navigate them**.

Even under oppression:
- Internal sovereignty protects identity
- Alignment reduces self-betrayal
- Coherence preserves dignity
- Regulated nervous systems prevent collapse

Historical examples:
- Enslaved people who maintained spiritual autonomy despite physical bondage
- Political prisoners who preserved mental clarity under torture
- Marginalized communities who built parallel economies when excluded from mainstream systems

Alignment is not a **substitute** for systemic change.
It is the **foundation** that makes sustained resistance possible.

Without internal sovereignty, external freedom collapses into new dependency.

Q: How is this different from self-help?
Self-help focuses on tactics and motivation.
This framework focuses on identity and infrastructure.

Self-help asks: *"What should I do?"*
This framework asks: *"Who am I being, and does my structure support it?"*

Self-help often produces:
- Temporary motivation
- Surface-level changes
- Guilt when tactics fail

Alignment produces:
- Sustained transformation
- Structural stability
- Clarity when old patterns resurface

Self-help is top-down (impose new behaviors).
Alignment is inside-out (rebuild the system).

Q: What if I try this and nothing changes?
Then you are likely:

A. Confusing insight with alignment
Understanding this framework is not the same as living it. Alignment requires **repetition**, not revelation.

B. Attempting change without nervous system regulation
If your body perceives growth as threat, it will resist—no matter how aligned your thoughts are.

C. Expecting instant results
Alignment compounds over time. Most people see shifts in weeks/months, not days.

D. Still operating from misaligned structures
You cannot build aligned identity while maintaining misaligned relationships, work, or environments. Something must shift.

If nothing changes after sustained practice (6+ months), reassess:

- Is your understanding accurate?
- Are you practicing daily?
- Is your environment too hostile for growth?
- Do you need support (therapy, mentorship, community)?

A Moment You Recognize
You asked the hard questions.
You didn't want easy answers.
You wanted **truth that could withstand scrutiny**.

Question:
What if skepticism was the beginning of alignment, not the enemy of it?

Recurring Question:
What if skepticism was the beginning of alignment, not the enemy of it?

PRACTICE FOR THE WEEK

Skeptical Self-Assessment
Write down your top **three doubts** about this framework.

For each doubt, ask:
1. What would convince me this is true or false?
2. Can I test this through my own experience?
3. What would change if this doubt was resolved?

Hold the questions. Let experience answer.

CHAPTER SUMMARY + KEY TERMS

CHAPTER SUMMARY

This chapter addresses common skepticism directly. Alignment is not positive thinking—it focuses on structure, not emotion. It does not guarantee success but increases probability. It does not blame strugglers but identifies structural conditions. It is not theology but analyzes theological patterns. It can be measured through trust velocity, decision clarity, and recovery speed. Divine language is used strategically to protect sovereignty. Alignment does not remove systemic barriers but changes how they are navigated. Unlike self-help, this framework rebuilds identity infrastructure rather than imposing tactics.

KEY TERMS

Structural Analysis — Examining conditions rather than assigning moral blame.

Probability Increase — Alignment raises likelihood of positive outcomes without guaranteeing them.

Trust Velocity — Speed of coordination enabled by coherence; measurable outcome.

Explanatory Divine Language — Sacred terms used to protect inner authority historically.

Functional Framework — Principles that work regardless of theological belief.

Inside-Out Transformation — Rebuilding system infrastructure rather than imposing surface behaviors.

QUICK SELF-CHECK

Reflect honestly:
1. What is my biggest doubt about this framework?
2. Can I test that doubt through my own experience?
3. What would change if alignment actually worked?

PRACTICE FOR THE WEEK

Write your **three biggest doubts**.
Identify how you could test each one.
Let experience be the evidence.

ONE-LINE PRINCIPLE

Skepticism is not the enemy—vagueness is.

PART VII:
UNLEARNING, TRUST, AND FREEDOM

Outgrowing Survival Frameworks

CHAPTER 16

"Survival wisdom is not the same as freedom truth."

WHAT WE WERE TAUGHT TO TRUST

Every community survives by teaching its children what to trust.
Trust your elders.
Trust your faith.
Trust hard work.
Trust obedience.
Trust patience.
Trust sacrifice.

For Black people especially, these were not abstract values. They were **survival strategies** passed down through violence, scarcity, and exclusion.

They were not lies.
They were **adaptations**.

But adaptation is not the same as truth.

What kept people alive under one set of conditions does not always make them whole under another. This chapter is not about blame. It is about **context**.

Survival Teachings vs. Liberation Outcomes

Many inherited teachings were designed to:

- Help people endure
- Help them avoid punishment
- Help them stay safe
- Help them belong

So they emphasized:
- Humility over authorship
- Patience over agency
- Obedience over discernment
- Endurance over alignment

They were protective.

But **protection and freedom are not the same thing**.

Wholeness, Perfection, and the Limits of Survival Teaching

One of the most effective survival teachings ever passed down is the phrase:

"No one is perfect."

It is offered as comfort, humility, and realism—and within a survival context, it makes sense. When the goal is endurance rather than expansion, perfection feels dangerous. It invites scrutiny. It attracts attention. It risks punishment.

So survival wisdom teaches us to lower our expectations of ourselves, to stay modest, to avoid claiming completeness.

In that sense, the phrase protected people.

But protection is not the same as liberation.

Here is the double meaning—the double entendre—hidden in the phrase:

On one level, it is true: no human being is without flaws, mistakes, or areas of growth. We are finite, learning, and evolving.

But on another level, the phrase quietly redefines **perfection** as something rigid, unattainable, and unrealistic—something no one should seek.

That is the sleight of hand.

Because the dictionary definition of *perfection* is not flawlessness; it is:

"The state of being complete, whole, lacking nothing essential."

Survival teaching collapses perfection into impossibility.
Liberation restores it as **wholeness**.

What survival culture never had the luxury to teach is that flaws do not negate wholeness.

Fragmentation does.

A person who is honest about their limits, aligned in their values, regulated in their nervous system, and integrated in their identity is **whole**—even while still learning.

Liberation outcomes are not produced by pretending to be flawless; they are produced by refusing to live divided.

Survival says: *"Lower the standard so you don't get hurt."*
Liberation says: *"Raise the internal order so you can hold more."*

The problem is not imperfection; the problem is fragmentation—when parts of the self are disowned, suppressed, or at war with one another. That is what keeps people from alignment, not the existence of mistakes.

Wholeness is not something you are born with or denied forever. It is something you assemble—through alignment, regulation, connection, and truth.

And once a person becomes whole, perfection is no longer an impossible standard imposed from outside. It becomes a **lived reality from within**.

This is where perfection becomes not a threat, but a destination. Not perfection as performance, but perfection as alignment. Not a static state, but a regulated, coherent one.

Survival taught us that seeking wholeness was arrogance. Liberation reveals it as **responsibility**.

Because once a person becomes whole—internally ordered, self-governing, and connected—life no longer fractures them at every opportunity.

They are not without flaws.
But they are no longer at war with themselves.

And that is what survival could never afford to promise, but liberation requires us to pursue.

Not flawless, but integrated.
Not frozen, but ordered.
Not superior, but complete.

The lie was never that we have flaws.
The lie was that flaws make wholeness unattainable.

They do not.

When Trust Becomes a Ceiling
A teaching becomes limiting when:

- It discourages questioning
- It punishes self-trust
- It frames desire as danger
- It equates suffering with virtue

At that point, trust becomes a ceiling.

People begin to feel guilt when they want more peace.
Suspicion when ease arrives.
Shame when they outgrow old containers.

Not because growth is wrong—
but because **the framework was never meant to carry it**.

Why This Feels Like Betrayal
Questioning inherited teachings can feel like betrayal of:

- Parents who sacrificed
- Elders who endured
- Ancestors who survived

But survival is not the final goal of any lineage.
Inheritance is.

Honoring what kept people alive does not require freezing ourselves inside it.

Growth does not dishonor sacrifice.
It **completes** it.

The Difference Between Respect and Replication
Respect says: *"I see why this mattered."*
Replication says: *"I must live this forever."*

You can honor elders without reproducing their constraints. You can love faith without outsourcing authority to its institutions. You can carry culture forward **without carrying wounds unchanged**.

A Moment You Recognize
You honored what kept your family standing.
You just didn't want to stay bent forever.

Question:
What if what you were taught to trust was never designed to make you whole?

Recurring Question:
What if what you were taught to trust was never designed to make you whole?

Practice for the Week

Inherited Belief Inventory

Identify **three beliefs** you inherited about:
- Work
- Money
- Success
- Rest
- Worthiness

For each, ask:
1. Was this designed for survival or freedom?
2. Does this still serve me, or does it limit me?

3. What would I choose if I trusted myself completely?

Write the answers. Hold them without judgment.

CHAPTER SUMMARY + KEY TERMS

CHAPTER SUMMARY

Survival teachings were protective adaptations, not permanent truth. Many inherited values prioritized endurance, obedience, and humility because those traits reduced risk under oppression. Liberation requires a different internal structure: discernment, self-trust, and wholeness. "No one is perfect" protected people in survival mode, but liberation restores perfection as completeness—wholeness without fragmentation. Respect for elders does not require replication of constraints. Growth does not dishonor sacrifice; it completes it.

KEY TERMS

Survival Wisdom — Adaptations designed for endurance under threat.

Freedom Truth — Principles that support wholeness and authorship.

Fragmentation — Internal division that blocks alignment more than flaws do.

Respect vs. Replication — Honoring the past without freezing inside it.

Wholeness (Perfection) — Completeness, lacking nothing essential; integrated identity.

Trust as Ceiling — When inherited teachings limit growth rather than protect it.

QUICK SELF-CHECK

Answer honestly:
1. What belief did I inherit that no longer serves me?
2. Where do I feel guilty for wanting more peace?
3. What would change if I trusted myself as much as I trust what I was taught?

PRACTICE FOR THE WEEK
Complete the **Inherited Belief Inventory**.
Identify: survival vs. freedom orientation.
Hold without judgment.

ONE-LINE PRINCIPLE
Survival wisdom protected you. Freedom truth completes you.

PART VII:
UNLEARNING, TRUST, AND FREEDOM (CONTINUED)

CHAPTER 17

"Freedom is an outcome, not a promise."

WHAT ACTUALLY PRODUCES FREEDOM

Freedom is not produced by belief alone.
If it were, the most faithful people would be the most free.
But across communities and history, a different pattern appears.

Freedom correlates more strongly with:
- Self-trust
- Internal coherence
- Boundary clarity
- Relational alignment
- Authorship of one's life

These qualities are rarely taught directly—especially to people whose labor and obedience benefited systems more than their freedom did.

FREEDOM AS AN OUTCOME, NOT A PROMISE

Freedom shows up as:
- Calm decision-making
- Reduced fear around opportunity
- The ability to say no without collapse
- Relationships that feel reciprocal
- Work that aligns with values

These are not rewards granted from outside.
They are **outcomes of internal structure**.

This is why two people can believe the same things and live radically different lives.

Belief does not govern behavior.
Identity does.

The Subtle Shift That Changes Everything
Most people were taught:

"If you believe correctly, life will change."

Freedom emerges when the sequence reverses:

"When you live in alignment, belief reorganizes naturally."

This is not rebellion against faith.
It is faith **embodied**.

Scripture never separated truth from action:

"Faith without works is dead." — James 2:26

Not because works earn salvation, but because **aligned action proves internal transformation**.

You cannot claim to trust God while living in constant fear.
You cannot claim self-worth while betraying yourself daily.
You cannot claim freedom while remaining internally imprisoned.

Freedom is not what you profess.
Freedom is **what your life consistently demonstrates**.

Why Reclamation Works Better Than Rejection

Rejection keeps you oriented around what you are leaving.

Reclamation orients you toward what you are **keeping and refining**.

Reclamation asks:
- What still serves life?
- What still produces dignity?
- What still supports coherence?

And just as importantly:
- What no longer does?

This honors lineage while allowing evolution.

It is how cultures stay alive rather than fossilized.

Examples of reclamation:
Reject: "Religion oppressed us, so I reject all spirituality."
Reclaim: "Institutions controlled spirituality, so I restore it to its original function—internal sovereignty."

Reject: "My parents' teachings held me back, so I abandon everything they taught."
Reclaim: "My parents taught survival. I honor that while building for freedom."

Reject: "The system is broken, so I withdraw completely."
Reclaim: "The system is broken, so I build parallel structures rooted in alignment."

Rejection isolates.
Reclamation connects.

FREEDOM WITHOUT CONTEMPT

The goal is not to make readers angry at their upbringing.
Anger can wake people up—but it cannot stabilize them.
The goal is to produce **clarity without contempt**.

Clarity allows people to:
- Choose differently without hatred
- Grow without superiority
- Lead without domination
- Love their people without shrinking

That is mature liberation.

This is the difference between revolution and evolution:
Revolution burns down the old to build the new.
Evolution extracts what works, releases what doesn't, and builds forward.

Revolution is often necessary.
But evolution is what sustains.

This book teaches evolution.

The Cost of Remaining Unchanged
If you finish this book and do nothing, a predictable pattern will continue:

- You will know what alignment is—but not live it
- You will recognize sovereignty—but not claim it
- You will see the contradictions—but not resolve them
- You will want freedom—but not build the structure that holds it

Knowledge without action is not power.
It is **intellectual decoration**.

The real question is not *"Do I understand this?"*

The real question is:

"Will I live this?"

Because alignment is not a concept to admire.
It is a standard to **embody**.

What Changes When You Commit
When you commit to alignment—not as ideology, but as daily practice—predictable shifts occur:

Month 1:
- Decisions feel lighter
- Energy stabilizes
- You stop over-explaining

Month 3:
- Relationships adjust (some deepen, some fade)
- Opportunities feel more aligned
- Money becomes less emotionally charged

Month 6:
- Your presence changes (people notice without you announcing it)
- Boundaries hold without effort
- Work feels like extension, not extraction

Year 1:
- Life looks fundamentally different
- Not because everything changed externally
- But because **you stopped leaking internally**

Year 3:
- You become unrecognizable to your former self
- Not louder—**clearer**
- Not harder—**steadier**
- Not performing—**integrated**

This is not exaggeration.
This is pattern.

Alignment compounds.

The Recurring Question (Final Return)
Throughout this book, one question has returned in different forms:

What if what you were taught to trust was never designed to make you whole?

Now the question evolves:

What if you are now qualified to design what you trust?
Not because you are superior.
Not because you rejected everything.

But because:
- You examined the frameworks
- You tested them against your life
- You kept what served
- You released what limited
- You rebuilt from clarity

You are not abandoning your lineage.
You are **completing it**.

A Moment You Recognize

You stood at the edge of something new.
Not rebellion.
Not escape.
Authorship.

Final Question:
What if freedom was always one decision away—the decision to trust yourself?

Recurring Question:
What if freedom was always one decision away—the decision to trust yourself?

PRACTICE FOR THE WEEK
The Commitment Declaration
Write this down. Date it. Sign it.

"I commit to living in alignment.

Not perfectly. Not instantly. But consistently.

I will:
- *Govern myself before demanding change from others*
- *Act from clarity, not fear*
- *Honor boundaries without apology*
- *Build what I want to see*
- *Trust what I know*

I am not seeking luxury.
I am reclaiming inheritance.

Signed: _____
Date: _____ "

Keep this where you can see it.

Not as motivation.
As **covenant**.

CHAPTER SUMMARY + KEY TERMS

CHAPTER SUMMARY

Freedom is not guaranteed by belief; it is produced by internal structure—self-trust, coherence, boundaries, and authorship. The sequence reverses: alignment stabilizes first, belief reorganizes second. Reclamation is stronger than rejection because it preserves what serves while releasing what limits. The aim is clarity without contempt: liberation that stabilizes rather than merely reacts. Knowledge without action is intellectual decoration. Alignment compounds over time, producing visible transformation within months and fundamental change within years. The final question shifts from "what was I taught?" to "what will I now choose to trust?"

KEY TERMS

Authorship — Designing one's life intentionally; the highest form of freedom.

Reclamation — Refining inherited frameworks without hatred; evolution over revolution.

Coherence — Identity and behavior aligned under pressure.

Mature Liberation — Freedom without contempt, power without domination.

Commitment Declaration — Written covenant to live in alignment; accountability tool.

Intellectual Decoration — Knowledge without application; understanding without embodiment.

Compounding Alignment — The exponential effect of consistent practice over time.

QUICK SELF-CHECK
Answer honestly:
1. What would change in my life if I committed to alignment for one year?
2. Where am I collecting knowledge without applying it?
3. What is one decision I can make today that reflects self-trust?

PRACTICE FOR THE WEEK
Write and sign the Commitment Declaration.
Post it where you'll see it daily.
Let it hold you accountable.

ONE-LINE PRINCIPLE
Freedom is not what you believe—it is what your life consistently demonstrates.

PART VIII:
UNION & CLOSURE

Recognition and Return

CHAPTER 18

"Recognition always comes before change."

THE MOMENTS WE RECOGNIZE

Most transformation does not begin with ideas.
It begins with recognition.

Not recognition of new information—but recognition of familiar moments that were never named.

This chapter does not explain.
It **remembers**.

A Classroom Moment
You raised your hand with a different answer.
The teacher corrected you gently and moved on.

You learned: curiosity was welcome, as long as it stayed within the frame.

What if what you were taught to trust was designed to produce correctness, not confidence?

Another Classroom Moment
You were praised for being quiet, helpful, well-behaved.
The loud confidence went to someone else.

You learned: excellence was safest when unobtrusive.

What if what you were taught to trust confused compliance with intelligence?

A CHURCH MOMENT

You were told to wait on God.
Desire became pride.
Impatience became lack of faith.

What if what you were taught to trust was meant to keep order, not develop discernment?

ANOTHER CHURCH MOMENT

You prayed for clarity.
Clarity required a boundary.
The boundary was called selfish.

What if what you were taught to trust honored sacrifice more than wholeness?

A FAMILY MOMENT

You were told: "Be grateful."
Gratitude became a way to silence disappointment.

Wanting more peace felt like betrayal.
What if what you were taught to trust was meant to help people endure, not evolve?

ANOTHER FAMILY MOMENT

You were praised for being strong.
No one asked if you were tired.

You learned: love arrived easier when you didn't need much.

What if what you were taught to trust rewarded resilience while ignoring cost?

A WORKPLACE MOMENT

You worked harder than required.
Your reliability became expectation.

When you asked for more, it felt like asking permission to breathe.

What if what you were taught to trust benefited systems more than your well-being?

ANOTHER WORKPLACE MOMENT

You were told to be patient.
The promotion went to someone louder, not clearer.

You wondered if alignment was invisible.

What if what you were taught to trust delayed authorship in the name of professionalism?

A RELATIONSHIP MOMENT

You explained yourself carefully.
You compromised generously.
You called it love—until you realized you were always the one adjusting.

What if what you were taught to trust equated peace with self-erasure?

A COMMUNITY MOMENT

You watched someone move differently—calmer, clearer, less apologetic.
People called them arrogant.

Quietly, you noticed life opening around them.

What if what you were taught to trust was unfamiliar with sovereignty?

THE MOMENT BENEATH ALL OF THEM

Many of us were taught to pray for opportunity,
then taught to feel guilty when it arrived
because it required us to choose ourselves.

That moment is not rebellion.
It is **recognition**.

A Final Moment (The One That Brought You Here)

You read something—a sentence, a paragraph, a chapter—and something inside you **shifted**.

Not because you learned something new.
But because you recognized something **true**.

You saw your life in these pages.
You saw the pattern you've been living.
You saw the structure beneath the struggle.

And for the first time, you didn't feel broken.
You felt **misaligned**.

And misalignment can be corrected.

CLOSING REFLECTION

These moments are not evidence that your teachers failed you. They are evidence that **you outgrew the frame**.

You are not wrong for noticing the tension.
You are not ungrateful for naming it.
You are not disloyal for asking what comes next.

The question returns—not as accusation, but as invitation:

What if what you were taught to trust was never designed to make you whole—
and you are now allowed to trust something deeper?

This book does not answer that question for you.

It simply gives you permission
to stop ignoring it.

CHAPTER SUMMARY + KEY TERMS

CHAPTER SUMMARY

Transformation begins with recognition: lived moments where compliance was rewarded, self-trust was discouraged, and sovereignty felt unfamiliar. These memories are not indictments of elders; they are evidence of outgrowing frameworks designed for endurance rather than wholeness. Recognition is not rebellion. It is the beginning of authorship. The chapter closes by affirming that readers are not broken—they are misaligned. And misalignment can be corrected.

KEY TERMS

Recognition — Naming what has been lived but not interpreted.

Frame — A system of expectations that limits sovereignty.

Self-Erasure — Peace purchased through abandoning self.

Invitation — The shift from accusation to authorship.

Misalignment vs. Brokenness — A structural condition (correctable) vs. a moral failure (permanent).

REFLECTION QUESTION
Which moment in this chapter made me pause?

RECURRING QUESTION:
Which moment in your life made you pause and recognize the pattern?

EPILOGUE

What Was Always True
This book did not promise miracles.
It revealed **mechanics**.

It did not replace faith.
It restored **responsibility**.

It did not elevate people above others.
It returned people to **themselves**.

What You Now Know
You now understand that:

Luxury is not excess—it is sovereignty stabilized.

Sovereignty is not arrogance—it is internal governance.

Alignment is not rigidity—it is coherence between who you are and how you live.

Fear is not wisdom—it is a tool that loses power when identity is clear.

Permission is not required—authority begins internally.

Money follows alignment—it does not create it.

Community multiplies what individuals begin—but only when coherence is high.

Women are source—not supplement.
Men are direction—not origin.
Freedom is earned through structure—not granted through belief.

What Changes Now
If you close this book and nothing changes, that is a choice.

But if you choose differently—if you commit to alignment as a daily practice—everything downstream shifts.

Not overnight.
Not magically.
But **inevitably**.

Because reality does not respond to wishes.
It responds to structure.

And when structure stabilizes, outcomes become predictable.

The Standard You Now Carry
You are now responsible for what you know.

You cannot unknow:
- That fear was taught
- That authority was outsourced
- That luxury is sovereignty
- That alignment precedes outcome
- That you are qualified to set the standard

This knowledge is not a burden.
It is **activation**.

You are not seeking luxury.
You are **reclaiming inheritance**.

And inheritance does not announce itself.
It simply **stands**.

A FINAL WORD

Many will read this book and admire it.
Few will live it.

The difference between admiration and embodiment is **practice**.

Alignment is not a philosophy to discuss.
It is a standard to **occupy**.

If you occupy it:
- Your presence will shift
- Your decisions will clarify
- Your relationships will adjust
- Your resources will respond
- Your peace will stabilize

Not because you demanded it.
But because you became **structurally compatible** with it.

THE WORK CONTINUES

This book is not the end.
It is an **entry point**.

The Luxorae™ framework will continue to evolve—through workshops, communities, tools, and practices designed to support those committed to living in alignment.

But the work begins with you.

Alone first.
Then in relationship.
Then in community.
Then across generations.

This is how inheritance moves.

What You Were Always Meant to Remember
You were never broken.
You were **misaligned**.

You were never lacking.
You were **disconnected** from your authority.

You were never unworthy.
You were **conditioned** to believe you were.

And now you know better.
So now you can choose better.

Not louder.
Clearer.

Not harder.
Steadier.

Not performing.
Integrated.

The Last Line
Luxury was never something you chase.

Luxury is what your life becomes
when you stop arguing with yourself.

RITUAL-FREE CLOSING PRACTICE

The Alignment Check
This is not a prayer.
Not an affirmation.
Not a ceremony.

Just a **daily alignment practice**.

At the end of each day, ask:
1. Where did my actions match my values today?
2. Where did fear override clarity?
3. What boundary protected my energy?
4. What relationship felt mutually nourishing?
5. What would alignment look like tomorrow—practically?

No judgment.
No emotion management.
Just truth.

Consistency here does more than any ritual.

Write the answers briefly. Track the pattern over time.
This is how identity stabilizes.
This is how sovereignty compounds.
This is how luxury becomes ordinary.

WORKBOOK

Luxury Is Sovereignty — Applied
This workbook is not about motivation.
It is about **stabilization**.

Use it slowly.

SECTION 1: INTERNAL ORDER

Exercise 1: Identify Friction
List three areas where your words and actions do not match.

What I say I value:
1.
2.
3.

What my behavior shows:
1.
2.
3.

No judgment. Only accuracy.

EXERCISE 2: NERVOUS SYSTEM CHECK

Answer honestly:
- When things go well, do I relax or tighten?

___

___

___

- Do I associate success with safety or threat?

___

___

___

This determines what your body will allow.

SECTION 2: ALIGNMENT STATEMENTS (PRACTICE)

Write one alignment statement for each area:

Money:

___

___

___

Relationships:

_____

_____

_____

Work:

_____

_____

_____

Health:

_____

_____

_____

Time:

_____

_____

_____

Template: "I act in ways that support _____."

Read daily for one week **without adding outcomes**.

SECTION 3: AFFIRMATION (AFTER ALIGNMENT)

Once alignment feels stable, add one affirmation per area.

Example: "I trust myself to steward what I build."

Money affirmation:

_____

_____

_____

Relationship affirmation:

_____

_____

_____

Work affirmation:

_____

_____

_____

Notice whether resistance appears.
If it does, return to alignment.

SECTION 4: MANIFESTATION (ALLOWANCE)

Do not declare outcomes.

Instead, observe:
- New behaviors
- New boundaries
- New opportunities

What appeared this week:
1.
2.
3.

Write what appears without forcing meaning.

_____

_____

_____

_____

SECTION 5: WEEKLY REVIEW

Ask:
- Where did I act from sovereignty this week?
- Where did fear make decisions for me?
- What felt easier once alignment was present?

CLOSING INSTRUCTION

Do not rush this process.

Alignment compounds quietly.
Results arrive loudly.

You are not behind.
You are building something stable.

MASTER APPENDIX

ESSENTIAL TERMS FOR COMPREHENSION

Alignment — Coherence between identity, values, actions, and boundaries.

Luxury — Ease, safety, clarity, and sustainability of life.

Sovereignty — Internal authority and self-governance.

Authorship — The ability to design one's life intentionally.

Polarity — Complementary differences that create balance.

Source — The origin of energy, life, or value.

Coherence — Consistency across inner and outer states.

Liberation — Movement from survival to authorship.

Community — A network that reinforces alignment.

Identity Infrastructure — The internal system that shapes outcomes.

Alignment Sovereignty — Self-governance rooted in coherence, not dominance.

Sacred Union — Right relationship between complementary forces.

Fear (Structural) — A conditioned state that disconnects individuals from internal authority.

Outsourced Authority — Deferring judgment to external systems while bearing consequences.

Fragmentation — Internal division that blocks alignment.

Load-Bearing Identity — The level of responsibility and abundance a person can sustain.

Nervous System Regulation — Establishing internal safety so growth no longer feels threatening.

Divine Feminine — Source function governing alignment, regulation, and continuity.

Divine Masculine — Direction, protection, and structure; extension of source energy.

Compounding Coherence — The exponential effect of sustained alignment over time.

COMPARATIVE APPENDIX

One Truth, Many Languages

Tradition	Core Teaching	Matches This Framework
Aristotle	Virtue is practiced identity	Alignment precedes outcome
Maslow	Self-transcendence > need fulfillment	Identity > desire
Bible	Kingdom within, renewal of mind	Internal governance
Bhagavad Gita	Action without attachment	Alignment before result

Tradition	Core Teaching	Matches This Framework
Christ teachings	Faith over fear, inner authority	Sovereignty without domination
Foucault	Power internalized through norms	Authority must be reclaimed
African Cosmology	Immanent divinity, relational sovereignty	Source + community = continuity
Stoicism	Mastery of self, alignment with nature	Internal order precedes external outcome

CONCLUSION:

Different cultures named the same mechanism.

Institutions adapted it.

You are restoring it.

APPENDIX C: NERVOUS SYSTEM FUNDAMENTALS FOR ALIGNMENT

WHY THIS MATTERS

You cannot align when your body is in survival mode.

This is not metaphor. It is biology.

The nervous system—specifically the autonomic nervous system—constantly scans your environment for safety or threat. This process, called **neuroception** (a term coined by Dr. Stephen Porges), happens below conscious awareness. Your body decides what feels possible before your mind gets involved.

When your nervous system perceives threat:
- Decision-making becomes reactive
- Identity feels unstable
- Boundaries collapse under pressure
- Alignment becomes physiologically inaccessible

When your nervous system feels safe:
- Clarity emerges naturally
- Identity stabilizes
- Boundaries hold effortlessly
- Alignment becomes the default state

This is why nervous system regulation is not optional self-care. **It is structural infrastructure.**

This appendix provides the fundamentals you need to understand and regulate your nervous system so that alignment—and therefore sovereignty—becomes physiologically possible.

SECTION 1: POLYVAGAL BASICS

The Three States of Your Nervous System
Dr. Stephen Porges' **Polyvagal Theory** identifies three nervous system states that govern how you show up in the world:

1. VENTRAL VAGAL (Safe & Social)

What it feels like:
- Calm, connected, present
- Open to learning and growth
- Able to think clearly and creatively
- Comfortable with eye contact and conversation

What's possible here:
- Aligned decision-making
- Authentic relationships
- Sustainable productivity
- Embodied sovereignty

This is the state where alignment happens.

2. SYMPATHETIC (Fight or Flight)

What it feels like:
- Anxious, agitated, hypervigilant

- Racing thoughts, urgency
- Difficulty sitting still
- Always "on," never resting

What shows up:
- Hustle culture as nervous system response
- Anger, irritability, control
- Overthinking, obsessive planning
- Constant motion to avoid feeling

You cannot align from here—only react.

3. DORSAL VAGAL (Freeze or Shutdown)

What it feels like:
- Numb, disconnected, dissociated
- Hopeless, depressed, collapsed
- Brain fog, difficulty concentrating
- "Checked out" even when physically present

What shows up:
- Procrastination, avoidance
- Emotional flatness
- Difficulty caring about outcomes
- Complete withdrawal

You cannot align from here—only survive.

THE KEY INSIGHT

You move between these states throughout the day—often unconsciously.
The goal is not to stay in ventral vagal 24/7 (unrealistic).
The goal is to **recognize which state you're in** and **return to regulation intentionally**.

Alignment Sovereignty requires the ability to self-regulate back to safety.

SECTION 2: RACIALIZED & INTERGENERATIONAL TRAUMA

Why Black Bodies Carry Different Nervous System Patterns
Slavery, Jim Crow, redlining, mass incarceration, and ongoing systemic violence did not just harm individuals.
They shaped nervous systems across generations.

This is not speculation. It is documented science.

EPIGENETIC TRAUMA

Research by **Dr. Rachel Yehuda** on Holocaust survivors' descendants showed that trauma can be passed down biologically—through changes in gene expression, not just learned behavior.

What this means:
- Your grandmother's terror during Jim Crow may live in your nervous system
- Your grandfather's hypervigilance under sharecropping may show up as your anxiety
- Chronic threat environments train bodies to expect danger—even when physically safe

This is not your fault. It is your inheritance.

White Body Supremacy Trauma (Resmaa Menakem)

In *My Grandmother's Hands*, therapist **Resmaa Menakem** names how white supremacy created trauma in three types of bodies:

1. **Black bodies** — Trauma from direct violence, dehumanization, and systemic oppression
2. **White bodies** — Trauma from perpetrating/witnessing violence; disconnection from humanity
3. **Police/blue bodies** — Trauma from being trained to perceive Black bodies as threat

The result:
Black people's nervous systems were conditioned to:
- Expect punishment for visibility
- Associate safety with smallness
- Interpret success as dangerous
- Remain hypervigilant even in rest

This is why "just think positively" doesn't work.
The body remembers what the mind tries to forget.

The Four Survival Responses
When threat is detected, the nervous system activates one of four survival strategies:

1. FIGHT

Looks like:
- Confrontation, anger, resistance
- Argumentativeness, defensiveness
- "I'll handle this by force"

In Black communities, often shows up as:
- Justified anger (righteous, necessary—but still dysregulation)
- Constantly "ready" for disrespect
- Exhausting vigilance disguised as strength

2. FLIGHT

Looks like:
- Avoidance, distraction, staying busy
- Overworking to escape feeling
- "I'll handle this by leaving/avoiding"

In Black communities, often shows up as:
- Hustle culture (constant motion to feel safe)
- Workaholism as identity
- Inability to rest without guilt

3. FREEZE

Looks like:
- Shutdown, numbness, paralysis
- Difficulty making decisions
- "I can't move, so I'll disappear"

In Black communities, often shows up as:
- Depression (often undiagnosed, untreated)
- Dissociation during stress
- Feeling "stuck" despite wanting change

4. FAWN (People-Pleasing)

Looks like:
- Over-accommodation, self-erasure
- Saying yes when you mean no
- "I'll handle this by making you happy"

In Black communities, often shows up as:
- Respectability politics (performing "goodness" for safety)

- Over-functioning at work/home
- Difficulty setting boundaries without guilt

The Point

Many behaviors labeled as "character flaws" are actually nervous system adaptations to chronic threat.
- Anger is not a moral failing—it's fight response
- Hustle is not ambition—it's flight response
- Depression is not weakness—it's freeze response
- People-pleasing is not kindness—it's fawn response

Alignment requires recognizing this without shame.
You are not broken.
Your nervous system learned to survive.
Now you can teach it to rest.

SECTION 3: REGULATION PRACTICES

How to Return Your Nervous System to Safety
These practices are evidence-based, somatic interventions used in trauma therapy. They work by signaling safety directly to your body—bypassing the thinking mind.

Use these daily. Regulation is not a one-time fix. It is infrastructure.

PRACTICE 1: GROUNDING (ORIENTING)

What it does: Brings you into the present moment; interrupts threat loops

How to do it:
1. Sit or stand comfortably
2. Slowly look around the room (don't rush)

3. Name out loud:
   - 5 things you see
   - 4 things you hear
   - 3 things you can touch
   - 2 things you smell
   - 1 thing you taste

4. Notice your breathing slow and your shoulders drop

When to use:
- Before important decisions
- After triggering conversations
- When anxiety spikes
- Anytime you feel "out of your body"

Why it works: Orienting to your environment tells your nervous system, *"I am here, now. I am safe."*

PRACTICE 2: VAGAL TONING (HUMMING/SINGING)

What it does: Activates the vagus nerve; signals safety directly to the body

How to do it:
1. Hum a simple tune (any melody) for 2-3 minutes
2. Or sing along to a song you love
3. Feel the vibration in your chest and throat
4. Notice your body softening

When to use:
- Morning routine (sets tone for the day)
- Before difficult conversations
- When feeling disconnected from yourself

Why it works: The vagus nerve runs through your vocal cords. Humming/singing stimulates it, activating the parasympathetic (rest) response.

PRACTICE 3: SHAKING/MOVEMENT RELEASE

What it does: Completes interrupted survival responses (animals shake after threat to discharge energy)

How to do it:
1. Stand with knees slightly bent
2. Start shaking your hands gently
3. Let the shake move up your arms, into your shoulders, then whole body
4. Continue for 2-5 minutes (longer if it feels good)
5. Slow down gradually; stand still and notice how you feel

When to use:
- After stressful events
- After conflict or difficult news
- When your body feels "stuck" or heavy
- Before bed (to release the day)

Why it works: Trauma gets "stuck" in the body as incomplete fight/flight energy. Shaking allows that energy to discharge safely.

PRACTICE 4: BILATERAL STIMULATION (BUTTERFLY HUG)

What it does: Calms the amygdala (brain's threat center); used in EMDR therapy

How to do it:
1. Cross your arms over your chest
2. Place hands on opposite shoulders

3. Alternate tapping: left shoulder, right shoulder, left, right
4. Use a slow, steady rhythm
5. Continue for 1-2 minutes while breathing slowly
6. Notice tension melting

When to use:
- During panic or overwhelm
- Before sleep (calms racing thoughts)
- After triggering memories surface

Why it works: Bilateral stimulation (alternating left-right input) helps the brain process and integrate stress, reducing emotional charge.

PRACTICE 5: CO-REGULATION (SAFE CONNECTION)

What it does: Nervous systems regulate through safe relationships (we are wired for connection)

How to do it:
1. Spend time with someone whose presence feels genuinely calming (not someone you perform for)
2. You don't need to talk—presence is enough
3. Eye contact, shared breathing, or simply sitting together
4. Notice your body relaxing in their presence

When to use:
- Regularly (community is regulation, not luxury)
- When you feel isolated or fragmented
- After hard days

Why it works: Humans are social creatures. A regulated nervous system in proximity helps *your* nervous system regulate. This is why aligned community matters.

PRACTICE 6: EXTENDED EXHALE BREATHING

What it does: Activates parasympathetic (rest) response; most accessible regulation tool

How to do it:
1. Inhale through your nose for 4 counts
2. Exhale through your mouth for 6-8 counts (exhale longer than inhale)
3. Repeat 10 times
4. Notice your heart rate slowing

When to use:
- Anytime, anywhere
- Before decisions
- During conflict
- When you can't do anything else

Why it works: Longer exhales activate the vagus nerve, signaling to your body that it's safe to rest.

SECTION 4: CONNECTION TO SOVEREIGNTY

Why Nervous System Regulation Is Not Optional

THE CHAIN:

Dysregulated nervous system
↓
Perceives growth as threat
↓
Makes fear-based decisions
↓
Fragments identity
↓
Collapses alignment

↓
Sabotages outcomes

Regulated nervous system
↓
Perceives safety in expansion
↓
Makes clarity-based decisions
↓
Stabilizes identity
↓
Sustains alignment
↓
Compounds outcomes

You Cannot:
- Trust yourself when your body perceives danger everywhere
- Make aligned choices when you're in fight/flight/freeze/fawn
- Sustain success when expansion registers as threat
- Build sovereignty when survival mode is your baseline
- Reclaim authority when your nervous system expects punishment for visibility

This is why nervous system regulation is infrastructure—not self-care, not luxury, not optional.

Regulation Is a Daily Practice
Like alignment itself, regulation is not a one-time fix.

It is a **practice**:
- Grounding when you notice dysregulation
- Breathing when decisions feel heavy
- Shaking when stress accumulates

- Connecting when isolation creeps in
- Humming when you wake up
- Tracking which state you're in throughout the day

THE MORE YOU PRACTICE, THE MORE YOUR NERVOUS SYSTEM LEARNS:

Sovereignty is safe.
Expansion is not dangerous.
Visibility does not equal punishment.
Success does not require collapse.

And once your body knows that—**alignment becomes inevitable.**

FINAL NOTE

Nervous system work is not about "fixing" yourself.

You are not broken.

Your body learned to survive under conditions that would break most people. That is strength.

Now you are teaching your body something new:

You are allowed to rest.
You are allowed to expand.
You are allowed to be whole.

This is how sovereignty becomes embodied.
This is how luxury emerges.
This is how alignment stabilizes.

Not through force.
Through regulation.

RECOMMENDED RESOURCES

For those who want to go deeper:

- **Stephen Porges** — *The Polyvagal Theory* (foundational neuroscience)
- **Bessel van der Kolk** — *The Body Keeps the Score* (trauma and healing)
- **Resmaa Menakem** — *My Grandmother's Hands* (racialized trauma, somatic abolitionism)
- **Deb Dana** — *The Polyvagal Theory in Therapy* (practical applications)
- **Peter Levine** — *Waking the Tiger* (Somatic Experiencing method)
- **Rachel Yehuda** — Research on epigenetic trauma transmission

FORMAL BIBLIOGRAPHY

Philosophy & Power
- Aristotle, *Nicomachean Ethics*
- Martin Heidegger, *Being and Time*
- Michel Foucault, *Discipline and Punish*

Psychology & Human Development
- Abraham Maslow, *Motivation and Personality*
- Carol Dweck, *Mindset: The New Psychology of Success*
- Bessel van der Kolk, *The Body Keeps the Score: Brain, Mind, and Body in the Healing of Trauma*
- Albert Bandura, *Self-Efficacy: The Exercise of Control*
- Peter Levine, *Waking the Tiger: Healing Trauma*

Neuroscience & Nervous System Regulation
- Stephen W. Porges, *The Polyvagal Theory: Neurophysiological Foundations of Emotions, Attachment, Communication, and Self-Regulation*
- Deb Dana, *The Polyvagal Theory in Therapy: Engaging the Rhythm of Regulation*
- Rachel Yehuda, "Intergenerational Transmission of Trauma Effects: Putative Role of Epigenetic Mechanisms" (Research Articles)
- Resmaa Menakem, *My Grandmother's Hands: Racialized Trauma and the Pathway to Mending Our Hearts and Bodies*

Theology & Liberation

- James H. Cone, *The Cross and the Lynching Tree*
- James Baldwin, *The Fire Next Time*
- *The Bible* (Proverbs, Hosea, Romans, Matthew, Luke, John)

Education & Social Theory
- Paulo Freire, *Pedagogy of the Oppressed*

Eastern Philosophy
- *Bhagavad Gita*

Black Liberation Thought
- Frederick Douglass, *Narrative of the Life of Frederick Douglass*
- Marcus Garvey, *Philosophy and Opinions*
- Malcolm X, *The Autobiography of Malcolm X*

African Spiritual Cosmology
- Traditional Yoruba, Igbo, and Kemetic spiritual frameworks

Contemporary Voices in Somatics & Embodiment
- Resmaa Menakem, *My Grandmother's Hands (listed again for emphasis on racialized trauma)*
- Gabor Maté, *In the Realm of Hungry Ghosts: Close Encounters with Addiction*
- Gabor Maté, *The Myth of Normal: Trauma, Illness, and Healing in a Toxic Culture*

Additional Resources Referenced
- bell hooks, *All About Love: New Visions*
- Audre Lorde, *Sister Outsider*
- Glennon Doyle, *Untamed*
- Brené Brown, *Daring Greatly*
- James Clear, *Atomic Habits*

ABOUT LUXORAE™

Luxorae™ is a framework, a philosophy, and a movement dedicated to restoring internal sovereignty as the foundation for sustainable freedom.

Born from the intersection of Black liberation theology, classical philosophy, nervous system science, and lived experience, Luxorae™ teaches that **luxury is not excess—it is alignment stabilized**.

This work exists to serve those who:
- Have outgrown survival frameworks
- Are ready to reclaim internal authority
- Seek freedom without self-betrayal
- Understand that sovereignty precedes provision

The Luxorae™ Framework continues through:
- Workshops and intensives
- Community practice groups
- Advanced alignment training
- Resources for educators, organizers, and leaders
- **For more information:**

Visit www.Luxoraelife.com

A FINAL INVITATION

If this book resonated, **do not keep it to yourself**.

Pass it to someone who is:
- Tired of performing
- Ready to trust themselves
- Willing to build differently
- Capable of holding more

This work spreads through **aligned circulation**, not mass marketing.

One person at a time.
One conversation at a time.
One decision at a time.

That is how movements actually move.

You are not seeking luxury.
You are reclaiming inheritance.

And inheritance does not announce itself.
It simply stands.

END OF THE LUXURY BIBLE

www.ingramcontent.com/pod-product-compliance
Lightning Source LLC
Chambersburg PA
CBHW020454030426
42337CB00011B/113